I Am …
and Yet
I Am Not

I Am …
And Yet
I Am Not

A Poetic Journey from Body to Soul

Authored By

ABHISHEK GARG

SUPREME PARINAMAN FOUNDATION

SUPREME PARINAMAN FOUNDATION

ISBN: 978-93-343-5318-1 (E-book)

ISBN: 978-93-343-3606-1 (Paper Back)

FOREWORD

By Dr. Yogendra Singh Rathore
NLP Master Practitioner | Founder – IWT Podcast | Times 40 Under 40

Some books inform. Some books inspire. But once in a rare while, a book awakens.

I Am and Yet I Am Not is one such soul-stirring piece of art.

This is not just a collection of poems or philosophical expressions—it is a gentle, powerful invitation to explore the self beyond the self. With every page, the author takes us on a contemplative journey that goes far beyond intellect and touches the very fabric of human consciousness.

The words within this book feel less like statements and more like echoes of inner truths—subtle reminders that there is more to us than names, roles, and identities. Through paradox, poetic depth, and spiritual resonance, the author challenges our rigid definitions of who we are and gently opens a door to experience what lies beyond form and thought.

As a transformational mentor who has worked with thousands on personal mastery and healing, I've witnessed the struggle people face in naming the "something more" they feel within. This book gives that feeling a voice. It speaks directly to the seeker, the silent soul who knows that beyond the noise of the world and the noise of the mind... lies stillness, wholeness, and awareness.

The elegance of this manuscript lies in its minimalism. Each line is infused with intentional silence. Each thought is an invitation—not to understand, but to experience. And that is rare.

To the reader: This is not a book to be rushed. It is one to sit with, breathe with, and return to. You may not "finish" it, but you will be transformed by it.

To the author: Thank you for your courage to write not from ego, but from essence. Your work reminds us that while words have limits, truth is limitless—and that truth lives within each of us.

Welcome to the journey within.

Dr. Yogendra Singh Rathore

DEDICATION

To my beloved **mother, Smt. Kanta Devi**,
To my dear **wife, Bhawna**,
To my precious **children, Anika and Adwit**,
To my wonderful **sister, Shikha**,
To my dearest **friends Ritesh Nishad, & Ravi**,
Above all, **to the Divine**, in every form and beyond all forms,

ACKNOWLEGEMENT

I am deeply grateful to the many individuals who have supported, guided, and encouraged me throughout the creation of I Am and Yet I Am Not. Without the help of these remarkable people, this book would not have been possible.

To my wife, who has been my pillar of strength and the driving force behind my every effort. Her patience and support have made this journey not only possible but meaningful.

To my cherished Friends, Nabanita, Sanjogeeta, Pavan, Tushar, whose presence, love, and camaraderie have consistently uplifted and illuminated my journey.

To my esteemed Life and Spiritual Mentors, Nikhil Bahel, Dr. YSR (Yogendra Singh Rathore), Swami Laxmandas Ji Maharaj, Premanand Ji Maharaj, Aravindaksha Madhav Das Prabhu, Buddhist Monk Sangha, Acharya Prashant, and countless others whose wisdom, love, and guidance have deeply shaped my inner growth and spiritual understanding.

To my readers, who are the heart of this journey. Your willingness to engage with these words, reflect upon them, and take the time to explore the depths of the message is the greatest reward for this book. I hope it finds a place within your heart, just as it has in mine.

To **God (The one and only who created us)**, whose divine presence has illuminated this path and whose guidance has been the constant thread weaving through every chapter of this book.

To those who have helped unknowingly — through their kindness, their actions, or even their energy — I acknowledge you with deep gratitude. You have contributed in ways unseen but never unappreciated.

To anyone whose name I have unintentionally omitted, know that your subtle and unseen support has profoundly influenced my path.

Special Thanks to my wife (Bhawna), my friends (Ravi and Ritesh), AI Tool (Chat GPT), and the team behind it who helped in crafting my words & emotions in poetic form.

Contents

Part - II

Part - III

INTRODUCTION

A Journey Back to the Silent Self

This is not just a book.
This is a doorway.
A mirror.
A breath.

It is not meant to be read like a textbook or studied like scripture. It is meant to be *felt* — like a long-lost memory that comes to you in the middle of a still night.

This is a book of poetry — but more than that, it is a book of presence. Each verse, each line, is an invitation to return:
from noise to silence,
from roles to essence,
from effort to being.

Why This Book Exists

In a world where everyone is becoming someone, this book invites you to become **no one** — and from there, to rediscover **everyone** you've ever been.

In modern life, we carry so much: Expectations we never chose

Titles that exhaust us A constant hum of "not enough"

And a heart that longs to rest We perform. We achieve. We belong.
But somewhere along the way — we lose the most honest version of ourselves. This book was born from that ache. And from the whisper that follows: "There must be more."

Common Struggles That Might Have Bring You Here

Most readers who reach for this book are not lost — they are **searching**.
They are not broken — they are tired of pretending to be whole.

You may relate to one or more of these: Feeling weighed down by the identity you're known for -

Longing for stillness, but unsure how to find it

Being surrounded by people, yet feeling unseen

Thinking deeply, but never quite touching the truth within

Wearing a strong face, while your soul quietly aches.If you've ever sat in a crowded room and yet deeply felt alone — this book is for you. If you've ever looked in the mirror and asked, "Who am I, really?" — this book is for you.

Misconceptions That Keep Us Stuck

Before diving in, let's release a few myths

You do not need to become more to be enough. Silence is not laziness — it is the language of the soul. Healing is not forgetting pain — it is learning to listen to it. You are not what you do. Not what you feel. Not what you think.

You are what remains when everything else is still.

What This Book Offers

This is a book of unmasking — but gently, with poetry and presence.

It moves through archetypes you've lived or will live:

The innocent child and the overthinking adult

The unseen lover and the silent teacher

The broken heart and the awakening soul

Each chapter is a mirror.
Each poem is a breath.

Each reflection is a gentle nudge to stop running, and just *be*. After every section, you will find self-reflection prompts and practices of stillness — not to force change, but to support uncovering what's already whole in you.

How to Use This Book

There is no single right way, but here is what I suggest:

Read slowly. Let each line echo.

Reflect — not intellectually, but intimately.

Pause where you feel resistance. That's often where the truth is.

Return to the parts that feel like home. Use the journaling and silence practices not as tasks — but as invitations**.** Don't rush. This book is not going anywhere. And neither are you.

What You May Discover

A deeper silence beneath your constant thoughts. Clarity about who you are, and who you are not. Freedom from identities you didn't choose

Peace that arises not from answers — but from *presence*

Why This Matters

The world doesn't need more perfection. It needs more presence.

It needs people who are willing to:

Walk gently

Love fully

Be real even when raw

Rest when tired

Lead from the soul, not from status

This book is a gentle beginning to that way of living.

A Whisper to You

You are not too far. You are not too late. You are not too broken.

You are already whole — simply covered in dust from a long journey.

So let these poems brush that dust away.
Let the silence between the lines speak louder than any sentence.

And if even one breath in this book brings you closer to your truth —
Then the purpose is fulfilled.

The Body's Burden

A journey through roles we carry, pain we ignore,
and strength we embody

The body is not just where life happens — it is where life *speaks.* Every role we play, every emotion we suppress, every truth we avoid — all of it leaves an imprint, not just on the mind, but on the body. We take birth, we live, and we die — again and again . Long after we've forgotten, the body remembers. Every smile we force, every truth we suppress, every expectation we carry, every failure we bury — all of it is quietly stored beneath the surface of our skin. Often we think of the body only in terms of appearance or health, but it also carries the emotional and energetic weight of our daily lives. It reacts not just to nutrition or rest, but to grief, guilt, ambition, fear, longing, and even love. We take birth, we live, and we die — not only once, but in subtle ways every single day. A part of us dies when innocence is lost, and something new is born when courage awakens. And in every transition, it is the body that absorbs the cost, even when the mind cannot fully process it. In the rush of our lives, we rarely stop to ask what the body might be holding — the tension in our back, the pressure in our chest, the tightness in our jaw, the fatigue that lingers even after rest. These are not random discomforts — they are signals. The body is not just a machine to be pushed or pampered; it is a sacred partner, a mirror of our inner world. This section — *The Body's Burden* — is an invitation to pause and listen to that mirror with care.

We are not here to diagnose or interpret every ache, but to simply bring awareness to the lived experience of being in a body. We will explore this through four key subtopics, each with its own reflective entry. ***Stages of Life*** looks at how our body changes and adapts as we move through different phases of being — from childhood wonder to elder wisdom. ***Relationships*** explores how the presence or absence of emotional connection can shape us physically — whether through the weight of responsibility, the softness of love, or **the heart's ache** of being unseen. ***Vocations and Archetypes*** reflects on how the roles we play — whether in our careers, families, or society — begin to mold our postures, energy, and even identity. And finally, ***Reflections*** offers space to inquire into what we've unknowingly carried, what we've denied, and what the body is ready to release. Each subpart will have its own introduction and guide to support your inner inquiry. But this beginning is important — to honor the body not as a burden we must overcome, but as a messenger we must finally hear. In stillness, awareness grows. And in awareness, even the heaviest burdens begin to shift.

Stages of Life

"Phases of becoming — from innocent wonder to weathered wisdom."

We take birth, we live, and we die — not just once, but in small ways every day. Life is a continuous unfolding — from birth to death, and everything in between. With each breath, something within us begins, ends, or transforms. Our body is not just a vessel but a sacred space where experiences shape us and stillness quietly awaits.

Before we begin our poetic walk through the different phases of life, it's important to pause and recognize that life is not just a linear path — it's a layered unfolding. From infancy to old age, we move through stages that shape how we see ourselves and how we relate to the world. Each stage comes with its own set of joys, challenges, inner questions, and unspoken longings.

We take birth, we live, and we die — not just at the physical level, but in small ways every day. The moment we leave childhood behind, something in us dies. The day we find our voice again, something is born. Life is constantly inviting us to let go of what no longer serves and step into who we are becoming.

In this journey, we often attach our identity to the outer roles we play — child, student, adult, parent, elder — but beneath all of them runs a deeper thread. These roles are meaningful, but they are not the whole truth. They are vehicles through which the soul expresses, learns, and evolves. If we pay attention, we'll notice that even in our most ordinary moments, there is a sacred rhythm — a quiet unfolding of presence through time.

This section is not a chronological timeline, nor is it a psychological theory. It is a reflective offering — a series of poetic glimpses into the inner landscape of each stage. It's an invitation to revisit your life not as a checklist of achievements or failures, but as a living, breathing expression of becoming.

As you read each poetic identity, allow yourself to remember, to feel, and perhaps even to re-meet parts of yourself you've forgotten. You are not just moving through life. Life is also moving through you — shaping you with each breath, and calling you home with every stage.

I am an infant... wrapped in breath
Before all words, before the mind,
I dwell in silence, soft and kind.
I speak in sighs the soul can hear,
A language lost, yet always near.
The world holds me in tender grace,
Yet I hold worlds—no time, no place.
Before all thought, before the seen,
I know the pulse of the Unseen.
Before I knew... I was the Known,
An echo born from Light alone..

I am a child... chasing meaning in the noise
I run through echoes, search through sound,
With sky-sized questions all around.
In tiny palms, I tried to hold
The mysteries the grown-ups told.
Sometimes lost in wonder's sea,
Sometimes left with just a "why" and me.
Yet laughter came with no clear cause,
And dreams would fly without a pause.
No need for reason, plan, or chart —
I lived the world with open heart.

I am a youth… fast and flaming
I burn with dreams not yet named,
Caught between wild and world-tamed.
They tell me "be this," "go that way,"
But I chase suns not built of clay.
I sprint through mirrors, break and mend,
Unsure where I begin or end.
Faces blur in the race to be,
Yet something truer stirs in me.
For even in wounds the world won't see,
I find a hidden map of me.

I am an adult… carrying calendars like chains
I walk in hours, boxed and planned,
A smile rehearsed, a task in hand.
My spirit stirs, too vast to cage,
While duty tightens like a stage.
Dreams call softly, out of view,
Through coffee steam or morning dew.
And yet — when no one calls my name,
I breathe… and life feels wide again.

I am an old… moving slowly, but seeing more

My steps are soft, my pace is slow,

Yet I behold what others throw.

The world runs fast, I let it fly —

For I have found the deeper sky.

What once I chased with urgent breath,

Now sits beside me still as death.

No words, no rush, no need to prove —

Just presence… pure, and quietly enough.

Relationships

"Ties of blood, bond, and choice that shape and shake our becoming."

Relationships shape our identity more than we realize. They hold love, tension, duty, and longing — sometimes all at once. Through others, we often discover hidden parts of ourselves. This section explores those connections and the lessons they offer.

Before we step into the poetic pages that explore our relationships, it's important to remember: relationships are not just external roles — they are internal landscapes. Every identity we hold in relation to another person — child, sibling, friend, partner, parent — carries its own tone, texture, and emotional truth.

We often enter relationships with expectations: to be loved, to be understood, to be needed. But we also bring wounds, stories, silence, and past impressions — sometimes from early life, sometimes from lifetimes of conditioning. These inner layers quietly shape how we relate, respond, and retreat.

This section of poetic reflections is not a celebration of ideal relationships — nor is it a critique. It is a soft unveiling of what we feel but often don't say. It gives voice to the invisible labor, the hidden ache, the silent loyalty, the unspoken gratitude, and the longing to be fully seen.

Each poem invites you to step into a specific role — not just to read it, but to feel it from the inside out. Notice what resonates. Notice what resists. These aren't just roles we perform — they're places where the soul tries to express through the human experience.

As you move through these pages, don't rush to label or interpret. Let each verse land like a whisper — gently,

honestly. These are not just poetic identities. They are mirrors, reminders, and sometimes, healing companions.

You may discover that in exploring your relationships with others, you begin to meet yourself more truly — not in perfection, but in presence.

I am an individual… lost in the crowd
I fade in faces, nameless, wide,
Yet find myself when none abide.
I walk alone — not out of pain,
But where I walk, I hear my name.
The night wraps tight in loneliness,
Yet I have learned the lamp's caress.
In hush that hums beyond the din,
I meet the One who dwells within.
Not the self the world has known,
But the one I left alone.

I am a son… born from blood
Raised on strength, taught not to cry,
To carry weight and never why.
They call me steady, firm, and bold —
Yet sometimes, I just want to be held.
On my shoulders, lineage rests,
But my soul too longs for gentle quests.
Not just duty, mask, or role —
But someone seen as living soul.

I am a daughter in Grace… adorned with hope
They dress me bright, they guard my way,
With love that watches night and day.
I bloom in gardens fenced with care,
Both lifted up… and held back there.
They see the softness, not the storm,
But I hold fire behind the form.
My silence isn't weak or small —
It's grace that chooses when to call.
Though shaped by fear and love's embrace,
I rise — not perfect, but in grace.
Not what they dream… but what I am.

I am a sister… a bridge between storm and still
I walk the line where calm begins,
Hold secrets soft beneath my skin.
I smile through blame, I bend with grace,
Often unseen — yet everyplace.
They lean on me, forget I break,
But I too ache for space to shake.
Not just thanked for holding tight,
But heard when I am losing light.

I am a brother... mischief, shield, and stone

I guard through jokes, I tease to care,

My love speaks loud in silent air.

Behind my grin, old wounds still stay,

But I protect them, laugh away.

My loyalty walks close, not loud,

I'm there — in silence, in the crowd.

They may not see how deep I feel,

But I'm the wall behind the wheel.

I am a life partner... strength and softness twined

I wipe their tears, hold dreams with hands,

Yet sometimes drown in love's demands.

I give and give, forget to rest,

While hiding rain within my chest.

I stay — not just when skies are clear,

But through the storms, I still draw near.

For love is not just felt — it's shown,

A vow that breathes when we feel alone.

I am a father with strength… a silent well of care
They see my hands that build and lift,
But not the cries I never sift.
I stand so others feel no fall,
Yet I too yearn to drop it all.
Love, for me, is steady feet,
That show up daily, firm and sweet.
I hold the weight, I hide the wear,
Still offering space with patient care.

I am a mother with care… womb of light and ache
They call me selfless, strong, and kind,
But they don't see the cracks behind.
I soothe the storms with steady grace,
While hiding tears I never face.
I pour love even when I'm dry,
Forget myself, but still supply.
Not just what I do — it's who I am,
A silent lamp, a giving dam..

I am a family soul… woven thread of home

I stretch, I bend, I hold the space,
In unshown acts, in silent grace.
They may not see the things I do,
But every light I leave is true.
In losing self, I somehow find,
A deeper love that stays behind.
Roots unseen that let them rise —
I am the thread that never dies.

I am a relative by blood… distant, yet known

We share old tales, and newer pain,
In silences that still remain.
We don't speak much — but when we do,
The heart remembers what is true.
Through festivals and missed replies,
A quiet love beneath still lies.
We may not meet, but we don't sever —
I'm still here. And I'll be — forever

I am a friend... chosen without blood
I walk beside, not in the light,
I stay when others take their flight.
I speak when needed, hush when not,
Remember all that you forgot.
I see the mask and love the soul,
I fill the gaps that others stole.
No score to keep, no need to win —
Just staying close is where I begin

I am a contributor in society... quiet, yet alive
I don't need fame to play my part,
I plant small seeds with steady heart.
A word, a gesture, unseen grace —
I help the world become a place.
Bridges I build are made of trust,
My actions small — but always just.
And though I stand without applause,
I breathe life into silent cause.

I am the pride of the nation... not by height, but by heart

Not because I stand above —

But rise when others need my love.

I walk with roots beneath my feet,

My breath — where ancestors and future meet.

Pride is not in boastful tone,

But in the truth I live alone.

In silent acts and honest grace,

I hold my land in every place.

With every step, I strive, not show —

A quiet flame in duty's glow.

For in my being, strong yet kind,

The light of Bharat gently shines.

Vocations & Archetypes

These represent societal roles, professions, and soul-driven callings:

Work is not just a way to earn, it's an expression of who we are. We step into many roles and archetypes in life, some chosen, some inherited. This section reflects on our deeper motivations behind action, and the journey from doing to meaning.

Before we enter the poetic expressions of roles and vocations, let us pause and acknowledge something deeper: we are not only what we do — but what we silently embody. Each role we take on in life carries with it a voice, a posture, a pattern of energy. These roles often begin as choices or responsibilities... but over time, they shape how we think, feel, and relate to ourselves and the world.

Whether we are caregivers, creators, protectors, teachers, servants, or leaders — every vocation reflects a certain **archetype** that lives within us. Some we embrace proudly. Others we carry out of duty. And a few we may even resent or forget we ever chose. But all of them leave their imprint — on our body, our identity, and our inner life.

This section is not about career paths or job titles. It is about the *soul behind the service.* These poetic reflections invite you to step into the deeper presence that exists beneath every role — to feel the longing, the sacrifice, the fatigue, the purpose, and the quiet truth that often goes unseen behind action.

Here, each poem becomes a mirror — not just to recognize the role you play in society, but to witness how that role has shaped your sense of self. Some parts may feel empowering; others may feel heavy or incomplete. That's okay. This is not a space for judgment. It's a space to breathe, reflect, and honor both the light and the weight of your lived experience.

Let each poetic identity awaken not just who you've been — but who you are becoming, when doing gives way to deeper being.

I am a player…Bruised by the game,
Lifted by the crowd.
I chase moments that vanish,
But their meaning stays.
I fall, rise, sweat, and strive —
Not for the trophy, but the truth found in play.
In fleeting cheers, I meet something eternal,
the rush, the rhythm, the fleeting dance.

I am a soldier …Not just of borders,
But of inner battles.
I wear silence like armor, duty like breath.
The world sees strength — I carry sacrifice.
Even in peace, I stand watch.
Because courage is not only in the war
It's in the wait too.

I am a teacher...I sow seeds
That bloom beyond my time.
I speak, knowing not all will hear now —
But someday, one line may change a life.
I give wisdom, but I keep learning.
Yet I know —
Truth dropped in silence grows deep roots.

I am an employee... Bound by structure,
Moved by dreams.
I clock in, but my soul still whispers.
They may measure my hours —
But my meaning lives in moments
no clock can track.
Even in routine, I carry purpose.

I am a doctor of cure…I touch the wound,
But speak to the soul.
My hands know the science —
My heart, the silence between pain and peace.
I cure with medicine… and presence.
Overwhelmed by others' pain,
Yet hold life sacred, even in exhaustion.
Even when the body breaks,
I protect the whole knowing God Heals.

I am a leader… in many roles…
Sometimes praised, sometimes blamed.
I hold vision in one hand, and
People's doubts in another.
I don't always know the way —
But I walk first,
So others may believe they can too.

I am a Guru…Not a voice above,
But a mirror within.
Servant of Truth –
Guiding the lost with roots from youth.
I don't give answers —
I awaken remembrance.
I walk behind you in silence,
Until you turn — and see your own light.

I am an artist…I paint what can't be spoken.
I see cracks as colors,
Silence as brushstroke.
While others chase perfection,
I celebrate what bleeds beauty.
I create — not to impress,
But to reveal.

I am a singer... Each note is a prayer.
I carry grief in melody and joy in breath.
Sometimes, my voice breaks —
And that's when truth enters.
I sing not just for ears,
But for hearts that forgot how to feel.

I am a writer...I bleed quietly into words.
Every sentence is a bandage,
Every pause a prayer.
I don't write to be heard —
I write to heal what was never said.

I am a healer…Not all healing is in medicine
Some is in presence.
I sit beside pain, not to fix, but to witness.
In my quiet, something shifts.
I don't always cure — but
I restore what was forgotten.

I am a nurse…I hold life at its
Weakest and strongest.
With hands tired but heart open,
I soothe the ache no one speaks of.
I serve without spotlight —
because comfort doesn't need applause,
Just presence.

I am an actor…I wear faces,
But seek my own.
On stage, I become everyone —
But inside, I ask: who am
I when the curtain falls?
Art is my disguise,
And truth, my stage.

I am a monk…in the marketplace of life
Searching for stillness in the noise and
Pause in the rush I wear
No caste but carry all paths.
My renunciation isn't escape — it's return.
Stillness is my revolution, and silence, my sermon.
Even in simplicity, I hold the whole universe.

I am a lawyer…I defend the unheard,
Even as doubt surrounds me.
I walk between law and truth —
Knowing sometimes they don't meet.
But still, I argue for hope,
Because justice begins with someone who believes.

I am a judge…Not just of law,
But of weight unseen.
I carry the burden of both proof and pause.
Behind every decision lies a heart too.
And though robes cover,
I never rule without soul.

I am a soldier / warrior…Whether

Battlefield or burden — I fight.

Not always with weapons, but with will.

I bleed in silence and stand for many.

I don't seek war —

But I won't run from what must be protected.

I am a guide /a coach /a mentor…

I walk beside, not ahead.

My job isn't to give the answer —

But to hold the mirror.

I remind others of what they already carry.

Growth begins not in advice,

But in presence.

I am a social worker…

I walk into places most avoid.

My heart breaks often — and that's how it stays soft.

I don't fix systems alone,

But I hold lives until

They can rise again.

I am a farmer…I work with the rhythm

The rhythm of rain and sun.

I feed the world and ask for little.

My hands crack, but I still sow hope.

And in the soil — I meet the sacred.

I am an artist / creator…

I shape from formlessness, make meaning out of mess.

I see what others step over — and turn it into light.

Creation is my devotion.

In colors, words, or clay —

I leave pieces of my soul.

I am a leader in politics…Voices clash around me

But I listen for the unheard.

I'm pulled by power, tested by truth.

Real leadership isn't popularity —

It's standing where justice shivers.

I don't lead for applause, but for change.

I am an entrepreneur / dream builder…
I chase visions no one else sees.
I fall more than I rise —but I rise anyway.
Success is a byproduct; purpose is the fire.
I don't build empires — I build possibilities.

I am a homemaker…They say "just at home" —
But I hold a universe between rooms.
My hands fold clothes and carry prayers.
In my silence, the family breathes.
Home isn't where I stay —
It's where I serve with invisible grace.

I am a nurturer…I give warmth — not as duty,
But as nature. I sense what others can't say.
In holding others, I don't disappear — I expand.
My care is a quiet revolution — one heartbeat at a time.

I am an astrologer…I read the language of stars,
Not to predict — but to reflect.
I don't tell the future —
I help you hear your own rhythm.
The sky isn't fate — it's a mirror of your becoming.

I am a doer… with mixed roles as servant.

Often unseen, yet unshaken,

I bow not because I am small,

But because I see something larger

I carry weight, unseen by most.

They see the task — not the soul inside.

But I serve not from lowliness,

But from quiet strength.

Even in the small, I move the sacred.

Reflection: The Body's Burden

The body is the doorway. Pain is not punishment, but purification.

What messages does your body carry that your mind refuses to hear?

Our body holds more than bones and breath — it holds memory, stress, emotion, and silence. Often, we overlook the body until it speaks through pain or fatigue. This section invites you to pause and listen to what your body has been quietly carrying.

As we close this poetic exploration of The Body's Burden, it's valuable to pause and reflect on the deeper threads connecting your personal journey to the shared human experience. Each poetic identity and role you have encountered—whether it felt intimately familiar or quietly distant—has gently invited you to notice not just what you carry, but how universally human these burdens are.

Your body holds not only your own unique stories, but echoes of the collective human story—of hope and struggle, joy and pain, belonging and isolation. Often, we mistakenly believe our burdens are ours alone, isolating ourselves in silence. Yet, in reading and recognizing these reflections, perhaps you have felt the relief of knowing that others, too, quietly carry similar tensions and truths beneath their daily lives.

Through gentle self-inquiry, these poems ask you: What am I holding within my body? What truths have I ignored, and what is ready to be acknowledged and released? The answers are not to be forced or rushed. They are to be felt, breathed into, and gently understood.

As you begin connecting more deeply with your own embodied experiences, something powerful happens: empathy awakens, bridging your inner world to the wider human family. You begin to realize that beneath the surface differences—age, background, culture, vocation—we share common struggles, common strengths, and common longing for wholeness.

May these reflections not only deepen your relationship with yourself but expand your compassion toward others. In recognizing your own burdens with honesty and care, you begin to see others more clearly and compassionately, realizing that we are all quietly carrying something unseen, yet profoundly human.

In this shared understanding lies healing—not just individually, but collectively. For when we honor the body's burden, we also honor the silent strength and dignity of every human being we meet..

Pause & Reflect Activity

Activity 1 – Listening to Your Body (Self):

- Sit quietly for 3–5 minutes, breathing gently.
- Notice your body without judgment: *Where do I feel tightness, heaviness, warmth, or ease?*
- Ask gently: *"What is my body trying to show or tell me right now?"*

- Write down any insights or sensations that arise.

Activity 2 – Seeing Humanity (Resonating with Others):

- Think of someone in your life you find challenging or distant.
- Reflect gently: *"What invisible burdens might they be carrying in their body?"*
- Consider: *"How might understanding this soften my approach to them?"*
- Note down any thoughts, feelings, or shifts in perspective.

Activity 3 – Shared Humanity (Collective Awareness):

- Reflect on the poetic roles and identities you read earlier. Choose one that deeply resonated.
- Ask yourself: *"How is this role or feeling a common human experience?"*
- Write down a brief statement, acknowledging and honoring this shared humanity.

The Fickle Mind

Wandering through thoughts, pressures, identities, and the quest to make sense of it all.

If the body carries what we do not speak, then the mind carries what we do not stop thinking. It is a restless companion — brilliant, curious, fearful, and often overactive. The mind is the storyteller within us: imagining, planning, comparing, analyzing, doubting, replaying. It moves between past and future, clings to identity, and resists uncertainty. It's not inherently wrong — the mind is a powerful tool. But when left unchecked or mistaken for who we are, it can become a cage we unknowingly live inside.

The mind wants control. It seeks clarity in chaos, even if it has to create a story that isn't fully true. It resists stillness because stillness threatens its role. It wants answers now, validation soon, and certainty always. One moment it's filled with hope, the next with fear. It can talk us into our highest dreams and talk us out of our deepest truths. This is the nature of the **fickle mind** — not evil, but unstable; not the enemy, but not the master either.

We live in a time of overstimulation — constant noise, endless choices, digital distractions. The mind feeds on this, becoming busier, louder, and more fragmented. We confuse mental activity with clarity, and emotional noise with intuition. We forget that awareness is something deeper — quieter, subtler, more spacious. The purpose of this section is not to control the mind, but to understand its patterns. To observe it without judgment. To realize that we are not the mind — we are the one who sees it flicker, who watches it jump, who feels its pull but does not need to follow.

In this section, *The Fickle Mind*, we begin by observing. Where does the mind go when it's idle? How do thoughts shape our sense of self? What emotions do we hold onto in thought form? Through gentle reflection, we invite the possibility of space — the space between thoughts, the space beyond stories. That space is awareness. That space is you.

The mind may be fickle, but it is not fixed. With attention, it can soften. With clarity, it can serve. With surrender, it can rest. And in that resting, we meet something deeper — not thought, not reaction, not belief — but presence. And perhaps, that's where real peace begins.

Thinkers & Learners

We process life through knowledge,

questioning, and observation

In the pursuit of knowledge, we often fill our minds but forget to quiet them. Learning is not just about information — it's about transformation. This section invites you to reflect on how thinking shapes your life, and how awareness reshapes it.

Before we step into the poetic pages that explore our relationship with knowledge, it's important to remember: thinking and learning are not just mental exercises — they are pathways into our inner world. Every idea we entertain, every skill we acquire, and every question we ask carries its own energy, shaping how we see ourselves and the world around us.

We often approach learning with expectations: to gain expertise, to prove ourselves, or to fill gaps in our understanding. Yet we also bring unexamined beliefs, inherited biases, and habits of mind that color every lesson and insight. These hidden patterns quietly influence what we notice, how we interpret, and when we choose to remain curious or close ourselves off.

This section of poetic reflections is not a celebration of intellect for its own sake — nor is it a critique of knowledge. It is a gentle unveiling of what it feels like to think, to question, and to learn from a deeper place. It gives voice to the restless questions, the silent breakthroughs, the doubts we hide, and the quiet satisfaction of sudden clarity.

Each poem invites you to step into a thinking or learning archetype — not just to read it, but to feel it resonate in your own mind and heart. Notice which verses ignite your curiosity, which stir resistance, and which open a stillness beyond thought. These are not just modes of mental activity — they are doors into awareness, each revealing a different shade of inner landscape.

As you move through these pages, resist the urge to judge your thoughts as right or wrong. Instead, allow each stanza to land like a raindrop on a pond, creating ripples of insight. These are not simply poetic portraits of the mind at work; they are mirrors, reminders, and sometimes invitations to approaches you've forgotten or never tried.

You may discover that in exploring your patterns of thought and habits of learning, you meet not only the mind's agility and restlessness but also the quiet observer that stands apart from both. In that meeting lies the possibility of true wisdom — not merely what we know, but how we learn to be with what we know.

I am a student... I gather books and break illusions.
I fail forward, not just to learn — but to unlearn.
Exams test my memory; life tests my presence.
I don't just study facts — I study myself,
One question, one stumble, one awakening at a time.

I am a traveler... collecting more questions
Than souvenirs.
Suitcase in hand, longing in heart.
I cross borders, but my real journey is within.
Every road teaches me to listen —
To silence, To strangers, To sky.
And sometimes, getting lost is how I return.

I am a seeker…thirsty beyond this world
My hunger is not of food, but of truth.
I follow stars and sages, temples and tears.
But every path bends inward.
I sought God in the sky —
Until I knew, and found Him within.

I am a philosopher…seeking meaning
I spin meaning from doubt,
And language from wonder.
I ask not to answer —
But to deepen the question.
Even silence is a thesis.
I do not teach what is —
I unfold what may be.

I am a scientist…seeking truth through pattern
Precision in hand, curiosity in soul.
I chase the unknown
Through equations and elements.
But even as I measure the stars —
I marvel at the breath that cannot be graphed.
Discovery, for me, is worship.

I am an innovator…ideas find me
At the edge of failure.
I imagine beyond limits,
Break what no one touches.
Sometimes misunderstood, often ahead —
I don't wait for approval,
I create the future.
In chaos, I invent hope.

I am an intellectual…I feast on thoughts,
Quote minds before me.
I hold logic like a lantern.
But when knowledge swells too high,
I remember — wisdom begins where knowing bows.
And even the sharpest mind kneels before wonder.

I am a researcher…I dig beneath surfaces
Where others stop.
Patience is my prayer.
Each failure a clue, each clue a step.
I seek the unseen not for power —
but because truth deserves to be found.

I am an observer…I speak little, see much.
I don't interfere — I interpret.
Moments pass others by,
But I catch the tremble in the hand,
The story in the eye.
Watching is not distance — it's devotion.

I am a doubter…I am the question
Beneath every answer.
Faith doesn't scare me — but blind faith does.
My doubt isn't rebellion — it's honesty.
I pull threads not to destroy,
But to see what still holds.

I am an analyst…I read between the lines,
Not above them.
Patterns speak — and I listen.
I see logic in chaos,
Find clarity in numbers.
But even I know —
Not everything meaningful can be measured.

I am a critic…I don't tear down — I reveal.
I question not to mock, but to sharpen.
Some truths need pressure to shine.
I may provoke — but only to protect what matters.
Skepticism is love wearing tough skin.

I am an explorer…Maps can’t hold me.
I go where questions lead and wonder calls.
Sometimes I find places —
Sometimes, I lose myself.
But each path carves me deeper.
And in the farthest distance,
I meet the nearest truth.

Masks We Wear

Roles adopted for survival, approval, or identity management:

We wear many masks — to fit in, to protect ourselves, to fulfill expectations. Sometimes we forget what's behind them. This section gently uncovers the patterns we hide behind and helps us reconnect with our authentic self..

Before we step into the poetic pages that explore our masks, it's important to remember: the faces we show the world are often not our true faces, but protective veils. Every mask—whether of strength, cheerfulness, competence, or indifference—serves a purpose, yet also conceals a part of our authentic self.

We learn these masks early—smiles to soothe, bravado to protect, silence to survive. Over time, they become so familiar that we forget there is anything hidden beneath. We wear them to fit in, to earn approval, to avoid pain, or simply out of habit. And while they can shield us from vulnerability, they can also prevent genuine connection, both with ourselves and with others.

This section of poetic reflections is not a condemnation of masks—nor an invitation to throw them away recklessly. Instead, it gently unveils what it feels like to move through life behind a mask: the effort it takes, the relief it sometimes brings, and the subtle loss of aliveness that can follow. These poems give voice to the tension between adaptation and authenticity, to the longing behind the façade, and to the unexpected freedom of letting our guard down.

Each poem invites you to step inside a particular mask—feel its contours, sense its weight, notice the shadows it casts. Pay attention to which verses resonate as familiar protection, which stir discomfort and which hint at a part of you yearning for truth. These are not just poetic descriptions of roles; they are invitations to explore how each mask has shaped your identity and relationships.

As you move through these pages, resist the temptation to judge your own or others' masks as "good" or "bad." Instead, allow each poem to land like a mirror—reflecting patterns of self-protection, patterns of performance, and the possibility of gentle unmasking. In that gentle unmasking lies the possibility of deeper self-awareness, connection, and compassion—both for yourself and for everyone who still wears a mask.

I am the actor of stories…I step into roles,
Recite scripts not written by me.
My face fits every scene,
But my soul remains backstage.
Applause feels warm —
But it fades fast.
Sometimes I wonder — when will I speak
Lines not rehearsed, but real?
When will I be seen without pretending?

I am the always-happy one…
The one who jokes, comforts, shines.
I smile so no one worries.
But my laughter hides a tired sigh.
Behind every "I'm fine" is a prayer:

I am the achiever…Goals
Are my compass, Success my second skin.
I move fast, rise higher —But rest feels like
weakness.
Sometimes, I reach the peak and feel… nothing.
I'm learning that being is as sacred as becoming.
And not every win needs a witness.

I am the caretaker…I hold
Everyone's pain in gentle hands.
I listen without interrupting,
give without asking.
But some nights, I sit alone — empty.
I'm learning it's not selfish to refill.
Because I cannot pour love from a drained heart.

I am the lone wolf…I walk
Alone not out of pride — but protection.
Solitude feels safer than misunderstood closeness.
I crave connection… yet shrink when it nears.
Still, under moonlight, I howl not for help —
But for remembrance: I, too, belong.

I am the perfectionist…
Edges scare me, flaws itch.
I repaint, rewrite, redo — again and again.
Even wins feel incomplete.
But now I see:
Imperfection isn't failure — it's life breathing freely.
I am learning to leave space
For the mess and the magic.

I am the strong one... The Reliable
The reliable, the rock, the silent fortress.
Everyone leans on me, but I have no one to fall into.
Tears hide behind "I got this."
I'm learning strength isn't just holding on —
It's knowing when to let go.

I am the peacemaker...
I smooth over tension, bridge the broken.
I nod when I want to scream.
Keeping peace outside costs war inside.
Now I know — harmony isn't the absence of noise,
But the presence of truth.

I am the clown…I make you laugh
So you don't see my ache.
I wear colors to cover the grey.
In jokes, I hide what hurts too much to say.
But every mask needs a rest —
Even mine.

I am the over thinker…I rewind,
I rewind, predict, analyze, repeat.
My mind builds stories faster than life
Can live them but peace feels distant.
But I'm learning — not every thought is truth,
And not every feeling needs fixing.
Sometimes, silence is the wisest answer.

I am the pleaser…I say yes
So they won't leave.
I mirror what they want,
Forget what I need.
Love feels earned, not given.
But I'm learning boundaries
Don't break love —they protect it.

I am the fixer…I rush to mend —
Broken people, messy moments.
Helping gives me purpose, but hides my panic.
If I'm not useful, am I still worthy?
Now I know: not everything needs repair —
Some things just need presence.

I am the "I'm fine" mask... Polished
On the outside, unraveling within.
I've mastered the art of pretending peace.
But silence grows heavy.
Now I ask — what if vulnerability is strength?
What if "I'm not okay" is the start of healing?

I am the rescuer...I jump into pain that's not mine.
I save to feel seen, to feel needed.
But sometimes, I drown in others' storms.
Now I know — love also lets go.
Empathy isn't enmeshment.

I am the performer…I shine under lights,

But dim when alone.

I live for applause —

Yet long to be held in silence.

I've played every role but mine.

Now I'm asking:

Who am I… when the stage is gone?

Inner Dialogues

Subtle identities or inner patterns that guide or distort perception

Inside us are many voices — doubt, hope, fear, wisdom — all speaking at once. These inner dialogues shape our choices and emotions. This section helps you identify those voices and learn how to listen with clarity and compassion.

Before we enter the poetic pages that explore our inner dialogues, it's important to remember: the conversations we carry inside are as real and influential as any spoken aloud. Every thought we entertain, every question we ask ourselves, every silent argument or self-encouragement shapes our mood, our choices, and our sense of who we are.

We often assume that our private thoughts are simply passing noise—minor distractions we can ignore. Yet those very voices—doubt, hope, criticism, compassion—steer much of our daily life. They color our perceptions, fuel our fears, and quietly reinforce our beliefs about what's possible. And because they seem so personal, we rarely consider how universal these internal conversations are.

This section of poetic reflections does not aim to "fix" your thoughts or to silence the chatter. Instead, it offers an invitation to listen more kindly and closely to the voices within. Through verse, you'll meet archetypal inner speakers—the skeptic, the cheerleader, the judge, the dreamer—and discover how each one plays a part in your inner landscape.

As you read each poem, notice which voice feels most familiar, which raises resistance, and which opens a window of calm.

These are not merely mental roles to categorize; they are facets of your experience—each carrying its own wisdom and its own blind spots.

Allow each poem to land like a gentle question: *Who am I when these voices arise? Which voice runs the show, and which one speaks from clarity?* In becoming aware of your inner dialogues, you gain the power to choose which voices to follow and which to observe without judgment.

In this exploration, you may find that the most profound dialogue is not between voices at all, but between them and the silent awareness that watches them pass. And in that space, true listening—and true freedom—can begin.

I Create, Nurture, End

I create, I nurture, and then I end,
My hands weave worlds, yet no one to defend.
I give and give, till there's nothing left,
In the quiet of endings, I feel bereft.
But from these ashes, new life will grow—
For what I end, another will sow.

I Rise with Courage...

I rise with courage, though trembling inside,
With every step forward, I try to hide.
The weight of my doubts, the fear in my chest,
But still, I stand—against all the rest.
I may fall, but I rise once again,
For in each struggle, I break every chain.

I Laugh in Presence

My laughter in the air, I'm present, I'm here,
Yet, I wonder—does the world truly hear?
I laugh for them, for all to see,
But the silence behind me speaks louder than me.
I long for moments where truth can be—
Where laughter flows, but I am truly free.

I am Present at Times

I show up when needed, in moments of grace,
Yet in silence, I hide from life's embrace.
Present at times, yet distant in thought,
I wonder if the present is what I sought.
In the stillness, I find who I am—
A soul searching, yet still holding the plan.

I Burn with Envy

I burn of envy, like a silent flame,
I watch as others rise to claim their name.
I ache for what they have and I don’t,
Yet in their success, my spirit won’t.
The burn will fade as I learn to see—
What’s meant for them, is not meant for me.

I Know Little

I know little, yet I seek it all,
In every answer, I find another wall.
I chase knowledge, truth, and light—
But in the end, the more I fight,
The more I learn that wisdom's grace—
Is found in knowing I must embrace the space.

I am Proud, Humble, Selfish, Selfless

Proud in my heart, humble in my mind,
Selfish at times, yet selfless I find.
I'm both the storm and the calm in the breeze,
A paradox tangled with conflicting pleas.
But in this balance, I learn who I am—
A soul in search of where I stand.

I am the Voice of Doubt

The voice of doubt, it whispers loud,
Filling my mind, hiding under the shroud.
It questions my worth, my place in this world,
A never-ending echo, like flags unfurled.
Yet I hear it and still, I rise—
For beyond the doubt, the truth lies.

I am the Voice of Fear

Fear grips my heart, whispers in the night,
It holds me back, steals my light.
It tells me I'm small, unworthy to try—
But I choose to challenge, to break that tie.
For in facing fear, I finally see—
The courage within is my true decree.

I am the Critic

The critic in me judges with harsh eyes,
Every flaw, every mistake, every rise.
I seek perfection, yet falter in view,
I tear myself down, though I know I'm true.
But I'll silence the critic, let love lead—
For the voice of judgment will never succeed.

I am the Inner Child

The child within me, wild and free,
She laughs, she dreams, she just wants to be.
But the world grows cold and lessons turn sharp—
And I wonder, does she still have her spark?
I'll find her again, I'll hold her tight—
For she is my heart, my light in the night.

I am the Inner Warrior

The warrior within, so fierce and bold,
She battles the world, both young and old.
With every fight, she learns and grows,
Her strength is built in the highs and lows.
She's not afraid of the road ahead,
For the warrior's heart is never misled.

I am the Questioner

I question the world, the why, the how,
Seeking answers, to the here and now.
I long for truth in every glance,
In every word, in every chance.
But some questions remain untold—
For in the asking, wisdom unfolds.

I am the Suppressed One

I am the one who hides in the shade,
My voice stifled, my truth delayed.
I carry the weight of untold dreams,
In silence, my spirit silently screams.
But no longer will I hide from the sun—
I'll rise, I'll speak, I'll be the one.

I am the Dreamer

The dreamer in me soars far and wide,
Chasing the stars, where hope resides.
But the world pulls me down with its cold, hard weight,
And I wonder if dreams will come too late.
Still, I dream, and in the dream, I see—
A world of possibility, waiting for me.

I am the Avoider

I avoid what hurts, what might break me apart,
I flee from the pain, I shield my heart.
But in avoidance, I lose the fight—
The courage to face what feels not right.
So I choose to step, to feel, to grow—
For healing comes when I allow it to flow.

I am the Observer

I stand back, I watch, I take it all in,
But I rarely engage, my world spins within.
I observe the chaos, the joy, the strife,
Yet I hold myself distant from the pulse of life.
But to live, I must step off the ledge—
Embrace the world, and make my pledge.

I am the Inner Judge

The inner judge, so cruel and sharp,
She strikes me down with a bitter remark.
She tells me I'm not good enough to win,
But I'll rise above, let love begin.
For judgment will never define my worth—
I am more than the story I birth.

I am the Unheard Voice

I am the voice that no one hears,
I whisper softly through the years.
My words are lost in the noise of the crowd,
But still, I speak, though my voice is bowed.
One day, they'll listen, they'll see my truth—
For silence only deepens the proof.

Reflections: The Fickle Mind

Thought is a tool — not the master.

What part of your identity have you mistaken as your essence?

When silence enters the mind, insight awakens.

The mind — sharp, swift, scattered — a master of disguises.

As we conclude this poetic exploration of *The Fickle Mind*, let us pause and reflect on how the mind shapes our everyday experiences and sense of self. The mind is incredibly powerful yet inherently unstable—always moving, constantly changing, and endlessly creating stories. It can lead us toward clarity or confusion, confidence or doubt, peace or anxiety, often in the same breath.

This restless nature of the mind is not a flaw to fight against, but a characteristic to observe. The purpose here is not to silence thoughts forcibly but to gently notice their patterns. To recognize that behind every thought is an emotion, behind every emotion a need, and behind every need—awareness itself. By becoming observers rather than reactors to our mental chatter, we begin to cultivate a sense of clarity and inner calm.

When you observe your thoughts without immediate judgment, you'll notice how transient they truly are. A fearful thought might arise and fade. A hopeful thought appears and passes. Even the most stubborn beliefs are fleeting when held lightly with awareness. It is only when we cling tightly to these thoughts—identifying ourselves entirely with them—that the mind becomes burdensome.

Through poetic reflection, you have seen various mental patterns—doubt, comparison, anxiety, ambition—each holding hidden messages and lessons. Remember, you are not these patterns; you are the spacious awareness that holds and observes them.

As you deepen your self-awareness, you might find compassion for yourself and empathy for others, recognizing the common human struggle with mental noise and distraction. We are all navigating similar inner terrains, seeking peace amid mental turbulence.

In this gentle act of observing rather than fighting, the mind's fickleness slowly becomes less daunting and more manageable. Clarity emerges naturally from acceptance. And in that clarity, something quieter and wiser within you begins to speak.

Pause & Reflect

Activity 1 – Watching Thoughts Pass (Self):

- Take five minutes to sit quietly. Close your eyes and observe your thoughts without judgment.

- Ask: *"What thoughts arise most frequently? Which thoughts feel heavy or urgent?"*
- Write down any patterns or observations that surface.

Activity 2 – Discovering Hidden Needs (Inner Awareness):

- Reflect on a recent challenging thought or worry.
- Gently inquire: *"What deeper emotion or need lies behind this thought?"*
- Write a few sentences capturing this deeper understanding.

Activity 3 – Compassion for Others (Resonating with Humanity):

- Think about someone whose actions or behavior you find confusing or frustrating.
- Reflect quietly: *"How might their fickle mind be influencing their behavior? How does knowing this shift my perspective?"*
- Note any new insights or softened feelings toward this person.

The Heart's Ache

Where emotions flood, relationships pulse, and longing craves its truth.

There is a kind of pain we don't always talk about — not physical, not mental, but deeply human. It lives in the chest, not as a sharp wound, but as a persistent tug. A longing. A quiet emptiness. A space that seems to ask for something more, even when everything seems fine on the surface. This is **the heart's ache** — the ache to feel held, to feel seen, to feel whole.

We experience this ache in many forms. It can show up as loneliness in a crowded room. As the sadness after reaching a goal that didn't fulfill us. As the gap between how we feel and what we show the world. The ache of the heart is not a flaw or a weakness. It is a signal. It tells us there's something deeper within us that has not been fully touched or understood.

The heart is the center of our emotional world. It carries our love, our grief, our hopes, our fears. And over time, it learns to guard itself — to protect us from pain. But in protecting us, it also closes itself off from true intimacy, vulnerability, and connection. The ache we feel is often the heart knocking from the inside, asking us to let it breathe again.

In this section, *The Heart's Ache*, we begin by simply acknowledging what we often suppress — the emotional weight we carry quietly. This is not a space for overanalyzing feelings or turning them into problems to fix. It is a space to pause and feel — without judgment.

To be honest about our longing, our sadness, our desire to be truly met — by another, by life, or by ourselves.

You may discover that the ache doesn't need to be solved — only heard. That beneath the ache is a deep sensitivity, a quiet wisdom, and a hidden strength. As you journey through this section, allow your heart to open — even just a little. Let it stretch without pressure. Let it speak without needing a solution.

For in listening to the heart, you may not find immediate answers — but you will begin to find yourself.

Feelers & Believers

Emotional souls who sense deeply and carry unseen inner truths

"Where emotion guides and faith finds its voice within."

Before we enter the poetic pages that explore our emotional depths and spiritual convictions, it's important to recognize: feelings and beliefs are twin currents that shape our inner world. Every surge of joy, wave of sorrow, flicker of hope, and leap of faith carries its own texture and power.

We often regard emotions as unpredictable tides to be managed, and beliefs as fixed truths to defend. Yet both are invitations: feelings teach us what matters most, and beliefs point us toward meaning beyond the visible. Beneath every strong conviction lies a tender heart; behind every intense emotion, a yearning for something real.

This section of poetic reflections does not aim to validate or invalidate any particular feeling or faith. Instead, it invites you to meet these currents with curiosity and compassion. Each poem offers a glimpse into the landscape of the sensitive and the spiritual: the feeling that wells up when beauty catches us off guard, the belief that lights our darkest nights, and the sacred tension between doubt and devotion.

As you read, notice which verses resonate as familiar comfort, which stir unrest, and which open a quiet Space beyond both emotion and creed. These are not simply portraits of feeling and faith—they are doorways into awareness, showing how vulnerability and conviction can become pathways to deeper self-understanding and connection with all life

I am a **Poet**

I am a poet, sensing worlds untold,
Through whispered verses, my heart unfolds.
I see what others fail to feel,
The emotions beneath what's real.
My words carry secrets, my ink bears pain—
An emotional soul, seeking to explain.

I am an **Empath**

I am the empath, with a heart that aches,
I sense the sorrows that others forsake.
Their truths lie in silence, too heavy to speak,
But I carry them, my spirit weak.
I feel deeply, yet remain unseen,
A soul that knows what others dream.

I am a **Faith-Holder**

I hold the faith, unseen yet pure,
In a world that doubts, I endure.
I sense the unseen path ahead,
The inner truths that others dread.
I walk with belief, yet question in fear—
Do I know enough, or is the truth unclear?

I am a **Devotee**

I am a devotee, who feels divine,
In every prayer, a deeper sign.
I sense the presence, though no eyes may see,
The truths hidden in simplicity.
I give my soul, but in silence, I wait—
Seeking the answer, while fate holds the gate.

I am a Believer in Beauty

I believe in beauty, in the unseen grace,
In the hidden truths that time cannot erase.
I sense the divine in the simplest sight,
In the unseen colors, the unseen light.
I carry this knowing, though others may not—
For beauty's truth lies in the quiet thought.

I am the One Who Feels "Too Much"

I feel too much, in every pulse and beat,
The hidden truths in every heat.
I sense the depths that no one speaks,
The quiet pain, the joy that peaks.
My heart is vast, yet too full to bear—
The truths I carry, hidden with care.

I am the Guardian of Others' Pain

I guard the pain, the quiet grief,
I sense their sorrow beyond belief.
The truths they carry, I silently bear,
Their unseen wounds, their unspoken prayer.
I feel their ache, their quiet plea—
And in my soul, their truth is free.

I am the Emotional Soul

I am the emotional soul, lost in the flow,
I sense what's unseen, what others don't know.
I carry the weight of the world in my heart,
Holding the truths that tear me apart.
But in this knowing, I rise above—
For the unseen truths are born of love.

Longings & Losses

States of emotional transformation and soul ache

"In every desire and departure, the soul discovers both ache and awakening."

Before we step into the poetic exploration of longings and losses, it's important to recognize how deeply these experiences shape our inner landscape. Every unfulfilled desire, every yearning for what might have been, and every pang of absence leaves an imprint on our heart and mind. Yet within these very tensions lie invitations to greater depth, compassion, and understanding.

Longings point us toward what gives life its flavor—connection, meaning, beauty—and they remind us of the gap between where we are and where we hope to be. Losses, on the other hand, puncture our certainty and dismantle the identities we've built around what we once held dear. Grief can feel overwhelming, but it also opens space for renewed perspective, tenderness, and the discovery of resilience we didn't know we had.

This section of poetic reflections is not meant to fix our desires or to resolve our grief, but to gently witness the full spectrum of absence and aspiration. Each poem becomes a mirror to the ache of wanting, the sorrow of letting go, and the subtle alchemy that transforms pain into presence. As you read, notice which verses stir a familiar longing, which evoke a fresh ache of loss, and which resonate as whispers of hope in the space between.Allow each poem to land softly—without forcing understanding or quick solutions. In holding both longing and loss with compassionate awareness, you may find that the soul's yearning becomes a gateway to greater acceptance, and that grief, held tenderly, reveals the depth of your own capacity to love.

I am with the Broken Heart
I wasn't shattered —I was softened.
Pain didn't destroy me,
It opened me to depth I never knew.
Now I bleed empathy,
Not because I'm whole,
But because I remember
What it means to ache.
Every scar is now a window
Through which love returns.

I am the Lover Who Stayed ..I stayed —
Through silences, seasons, self-forgetting.
I believed that presence saves what was slipping.
Even when I felt invisible, I remained.
Now I know: real love
Doesn't beg — it breathes.
And letting go not always mean run away
But a form of staying with myself.

I am the Mirror

I reflected their brilliance,
Their shadows, their becoming.
But rarely did anyone stop to ask
What I saw in mine.
They loved their reflection,
Not the mirror. Now I polish myself —
Not to reflect, but to shine from within.

I am the Memory Left Behind

I live in corners of old homes,
Familiar music, forgotten smells.
I am not a ghost —
I am what made the space feel like home.
They moved on, but I linger not to haunt…
but to remind them they once belonged.

I am the Pause in Prayer

There are no grand words, just breath.
In between thoughts, between wounds,
I kneel — not to ask, but to listen.
Sometimes, prayer is a pause
That holds the whole universe.
I don't speak — I become the silence.

I am the One Who Loved Deeply

I didn't love in parts — I gave all.
Even when I was unsure, afraid, or hurt,
I stayed true.
Now I carry stories in my ribs,
And stars in my eyes.
Deep love never leaves —
It becomes the light within.

I am the One Who Helped Others Rise

I gave my shoulders, my voice, my unseen tears.

They rose — and I stepped back without a name.

But I don't regret, for I rise in their rising.

I became the wind beneath wings —

Invisible, but essential.

I am the One Who Cried Alone

My tears made no sound,

But they softened the silence.

There was no hand to hold —So I held myself.

Not a weakness —

But a sacred rite of healing.

I cry not to fall apart,

But to come home.

I am the One Who Stayed Too Long

I waited in doorways

No one walked through anymore.

I kept showing up,

Hoping love would return.

But I vanished trying to matter.

Leaving became my rebirth —

Not out of anger, but of truth.

I am the Left Behind

No goodbye, just absence.

I kept replaying the last smile,

The half-spoken words. They moved on —

I stood still, aching.

But being left was a beginning —

Of finding my own voice again.

I am the One Who Let Go

I didn't walk away — I released.

Hands trembling, heart breaking,

I chose peace over pain.

Letting go wasn't weakness —It was wisdom.

Because staying where love is lost

Is its own kind of leaving.

I am the Unseen Mirror

I reflected their light, held their secrets,

Absorbed their pain.

They saw their best — and missed mine.

Now I stand not as a mirror…

But as a being worth seeing.

I am the Unspoken Goodbye

There was no closure —

Only fading presence.

I begged for clarity,

But silence stayed.

Now I close chapters in whispers,

And say goodbye not for them,

But to free myself.

I am **the One Who Loved Silently**

Every glance, every pause, every stayed

Breath was a confession.

But I never said the words —

I feared they'd vanish in air.

Now I know: unspoken love still shapes us…

But sometimes, it also breaks us.

I am the One Who Lost Faith

I believed with all I had —
Until the answers disappeared.
My prayers turned quiet,
My hope flickered.
But something deeper remained —
The yearning to believe again.
Losing faith was never the end —
It was an invitation to begin new.

I am the Abandoned Inner Child

Told to grow up too soon,
I buried play under pressure.
But beneath duty, a small voice still called.
I'm learning to return —
Not to relive, but to reclaim.
My healing began the moment
I held that forgotten child.

I am the Soul Searching for Union

I ache not for a person,
But for the Divine pulse.
In every lover, every silence, I've searched.
It's not romance I seek — it's reunion.
A sacred merging with something
That makes all pieces whole.

The Remembrance of What Was

Laughter faded, walls changed —
But memory remains fragrant.
I don't revisit to hurt — I return to remember.
Not all past is pain, some of it is a soft blessing
A reminder of who I was,
And what shaped me.

Reflection: The Heart's Ache

The heart holds no grudges — only echoes waiting to be heard.
What grief are you still naming love?

Let feeling flow through, not bury in. You are not your ache — but you are its home.

As we conclude this poetic exploration of *The Heart's Ache*, we gently step into the subtle and often vulnerable territory of our emotional landscape. Unlike the mind's quick, shifting thoughts or the body's tangible sensations, the heart speaks in quiet feelings—longings we might struggle to name, aches we silently carry, and desires we might not dare express openly.

This ache of the heart is universal. It arises not only from unfulfilled romantic love but from deeper longings—to be truly seen, deeply understood, genuinely accepted, and completely held. The heart's ache points toward unmet emotional needs, suppressed feelings, and unseen truths within us. Yet, it also contains seeds of profound compassion, sensitivity, and emotional wisdom.

When we pause to truly feel our heart's ache, we acknowledge the hidden vulnerabilities that connect us to each other. We realize we are not alone in this tenderness; everyone around us carries their own unspoken ache. In recognizing this, empathy arises naturally, bridging our emotional worlds.

Through the poetic reflections, you have touched various emotional truths, from silent loneliness to the longing for authentic connection.

By naming these feelings, you begin the process of emotional honesty and self-compassion. It's not always easy or comfortable, but it is deeply healing. As you continue this inner listening, remember that emotions are not problems to be solved—they are experiences to be gently witnessed. In witnessing the heart's ache without judgment or resistance, you open yourself to deeper emotional freedom, authentic connection, and unconditional self-acceptance.

Let this tenderness become a strength, not something you hide from, but something you carry openly, gently, and honestly—transforming ache into empathy, and longing into loving presence.

Pause & Reflect Activity

Activity 1 – Naming Your Ache (Self-Reflection):

- Sit quietly for 3–5 minutes, placing a gentle hand over your heart.
- Ask softly: *"What is my heart longing for right now?"*
- Write down your reflections honestly and gently, without judgment.

Activity 2 – Embracing Vulnerability (Inner Awareness):

- Reflect on a recent emotional experience where you felt unseen, unheard, or misunderstood.
- Gently inquire: *"What deeper emotional need was beneath this experience?"*
- Capture your insights in writing, allowing compassion for your vulnerability.

Activity 3 – Shared Compassion (Resonating with Humanity):

- Think of someone close to you who seems distant, withdrawn, or emotionally challenging.
- Ask yourself softly: *"What hidden ache or longing might they be carrying within their heart?"*
- Reflect briefly on how understanding their hidden pain shifts your feelings or approach toward them.

The Soul's Calling

Beyond roles, noise, and ache

— into the vastness of being.

There comes a moment — or a quiet series of moments — when all outer noise begins to fade, and something deeper starts to stir within. It doesn't arrive with fanfare or answers. It doesn't shout or insist. It whispers. It waits. It watches. This is **the soul's calling** — the subtle pull toward something true, something lasting, something beyond roles, goals, or recognition.

Many of us spend years living by what the world tells us is important — success, security, approval, image. And yet, despite doing "everything right," something inside still feels incomplete. That emptiness is not a failure. It's an invitation. It signals that we've outgrown the surface, and it's time to go inward. The soul does not speak in ambition — it speaks in alignment. It doesn't ask, *What should I do?* It asks, *Who am I, really? And what am I here to serve?*

Unlike the mind, the soul doesn't deal in logic or urgency. Its language is silence, longing, curiosity, resonance. You may feel it as a quiet discomfort in the life you've built, or a strange pull toward something uncertain but deeply familiar. It may show up in art, in nature, in grief, or in unexpected inner questions. The soul's calling often begins where control ends.

In this section, *The Soul's Calling*, we won't try to define the soul or reduce it to theory.

Instead, we allow space to listen. Not just with the ears, but with presence. We reflect on what calls us beyond comfort and identity. We explore how the soul reveals itself not through effort — but through surrender, honesty, and stillness.

There is no fixed path here, no guarantee of clarity. But there is a return — a remembering. A homecoming to what has always been within you, even before the world gave you a name. Your soul's calling is not another task to achieve — it is a direction to follow, quietly, faithfully, in your own way.

If the heart aches for connection, the soul yearns for truth. And when you begin to walk in tune with that truth, life stops being just a series of events… and becomes a living expression of your essence.

Beyond the Known

"Where the seeker dissolves and only presence remains — beyond maps, names, and seeking."

"Where certainty ends and the mystery of being begins."

Before we enter the poetic pages that explore the territory "Beyond Known," it's important to remember: life's deepest truths often lie outside the borders of our comfort and comprehension. Every moment we think we understand, the universe quietly expands, inviting us into uncharted realms of possibility.

This section of poetic reflections is not about providing answers or mapping every path. Instead, it opens a space for wonder, curiosity, and reverence for what we cannot yet name. Each poem serves as a lantern, illuminating the edges of our familiar world and beckoning us toward that spacious unknown where intuition, awe, and the sacred converge.

As you read, notice how certain verses stretch your sense of what's possible—how they stir a trembling question or a gentle thrill of recognition. Feel into the quiet tension between what you know and what you sense beneath it. These are not obstacles to overcome, but thresholds to cross.

Allow each poem to land like a star rising in the dusk—small at first, then burning brighter in your awareness. In this encounter with the Beyond Known, you may discover that the greatest adventure is not out there, but within: the unfolding of your own hidden capacities for wonder, silence, and deep belonging to a mystery that is both intimate and infinite.

I am the Wanderer of Inner Skies

I walk inner paths no map can hold.
Sometimes lost in light,
Sometimes wrapped in shadow.
But even the dark speaks
Wisdom in silence.
I keep walking, not to arrive,
But to remember
Who I am beyond the path.

I am the Silence Between My Names

I am not the label, the title, the task.

I am the breath before the word,

The space between identities.

Not empty — but infinite.

Not missing — but melted.

In stillness, I become whole again.

I am the Prayer Without Words

I rise from within,

Not to ask, but to offer.

My soul aches

Not for answers, but for connection.

No language needed — just presence.

In silence, I become prayer.

And in surrender, I return to the Divine.

I am the Seeker Who Became Still

I chased stars, followed teachings, wandered far.

But the more I sought,

The further I drifted.

Then came stillness —

Not as absence, but arrival.

Now I know:

I was never the one who seeks…

I was always the sky.

The Inner Witness

"The silent observer within — untouched, unchanging, ever-aware."

"The silent observer beyond thought, emotion, and form."

Before we enter the poetic pages that explore the Inner Witness, remember: there is a part of you that simply watches—without judgment, without agenda. While the mind churns, the heart aches, and the body aches, the Inner Witness remains calm and curious.

This section's verses don't ask you to change anything; they invite you to notice the space in which all experience arises. Each poem is a window into that ever-present awareness—showing you how to rest in the background of your own story. As you read, allow yourself to feel seen by this silent presence, and discover how abiding in it can transform every other part of your life.

I am the watcher behind the story...

I witness life without needing to control it.

I see pain without naming it wrong,

I see joy without clutching it tight.

In every fall, I rise — but never as before.

Because watching isn't escaping —

It's remembering: I am not the event,

But the awareness behind it.

I am the soul's whisper in the storm of doing...

When the world screams "more,

" I murmur "enough."

I speak in stillness, not in sound.

While others chase noise,

I breathe presence.

I am not a task, not a title —

But the hum that remains

When all else fades.

I am what holds you together.

I am the unlocked…

I no longer afraid of endings,
I have touched the space where nothing ends.
I've died a thousand small deaths and found
truth In each. Now I walk lighter —
Not because I lost, but because
I no longer cling. I am free.

Reflection: The Soul's Calling

The soul does not speak in logic, it sings in silence.
What is in you has never changed — even through all the changes?

When you stop being someone, you begin being everything.

As we conclude this poetic exploration of *The Soul's Calling*, we move gently into the subtle and sacred space where our deepest essence speaks. Unlike the body's tangible sensations, the mind's restless thoughts, or the heart's emotional waves, the soul communicates quietly—in subtle pulls, whispers of intuition, and moments of profound resonance.

The soul's calling is not something easily defined, explained, or chased. Rather, it's something gently uncovered, patiently heard, and softly honored. Often, we recognize it as a subtle restlessness—a feeling that something deeper within us longs for greater alignment, authenticity, or purpose.

Our society encourages us to pursue external achievements—status, success, security—but the soul's calling invites us inward. It's less concerned with what we accomplish and more with who we become. It urges us not toward ambition, but toward authenticity; not toward performance, but toward presence.

In this quiet inner listening, you've likely touched upon different aspects of your soul's voice: subtle longings, hidden talents, forgotten dreams, or gentle calls toward something meaningful. These poetic reflections are mirrors, inviting you to reconnect with your truest self—the self beyond roles, expectations, and identities.

Listening to the soul requires courage, patience, and trust. It often means stepping away from certainty and moving toward intuition. But in doing so, you become more aligned with your deepest nature. Life becomes less about achieving and more about expressing the essence of who you truly are.

As you continue this inner journey, allow your soul's calling to guide you—not with urgency or fear, but with curiosity, kindness, and faith. Your soul doesn't promise clarity immediately, but it gently assures you of alignment, inner peace, and deeper meaning The soul does not shout. But it never lies. It waits, patiently… until you are ready to listen..

In honoring this subtle inner voice, you begin not just to live—but to live authentically, embodying the quiet truth of your being in each step you take.

Pause & Reflect Activity

Activity 1 – Hearing Your Soul's Whisper (Self-Reflection):

- Sit quietly for a few minutes, closing your eyes and breathing slowly.
- Softly ask: *"What subtle inner call have I felt lately? What does my soul long to express?"*
- Write down whatever arises without censoring or judging.

Activity 2 – Signs of Alignment (Inner Awareness):

- Reflect on recent experiences where you felt deeply aligned, fulfilled, or quietly joyful.
- Ask gently: *"What were these moments showing me about my soul's calling?"*
- Capture insights and patterns you notice in these experiences.

Activity 3 – Honoring Others' Calling (Resonating with Humanity):

- Consider someone in your life who seems restless, lost, or searching for deeper meaning.
- Reflect compassionately: *"How might they be experiencing their own soul's calling?"*
- Note any insights or feelings of empathy that arise, and how you might gently support their journey

Beyond Identity

"The silent observer within — untouched, unchanging, ever-aware."

I am …Yet I am Not

I am many things…
Yet deeply, I am one.
I've been the moon's dance
And the sun's flame
Both fleeting and eternal.
But now… I feel, I'm no longer "me."
Somewhere along the way,
I lost the idea of who I used to be.
Yet the more I became —
In names, in roles, in doing —
The more I realized…
Being "nothing" is one of the deepest
And highest truths in the world.
For from nothing… everything flows.
I am not lost.
I am being reborn.

In this unraveling,
A truer me is rising —
Quietly, gently, powerfully.
I am peaceful… even when the world is not.
I am free… even when held tight by roles.
I accept… what is, without needing control.
I forgive… as carrying pain isn't mine to keep.
I only know love… and I give it selflessly.
I am satisfied… not because everything is perfect,
But because I've made
Peace with being imperfectly whole.

Reflective Glossary and Notes

"Not just meanings — they are echoes of the journey."

Glossary of Poetic Metaphors / Reflections

- Sky — the vast consciousness we belong to
- Mirror — the self as reflected through others
- Silence — truth beneath all words
- Wanderer/Seeker — the spiritual impulse in every being
- Light & Shadow — the seen and unseen within
- Home — not a place, but a state of soul-acceptance
- Body — Not merely flesh and function, but a temporary temple of transformation.
- Mind — A master when ruled by ego, a servant when guided by awareness.
- Heart — The silent bridge between suffering and surrender.
- Soul — Not born, not bound — simply remembered.
- Nothingness — The womb of all beginnings.
- Being — The essence beyond doing.

Self-Reflection Prompts

Each prompt a doorway
— not to know more, but to be more

We often ask others: *Who do you think I am?* But how often do we ask ourselves: *Who am I… when no one is watching?*

Self-reflection is not self-judgment. It is not a harsh interrogation. It is a soft inner gaze — curious, honest, unafraid. In a world obsessed with answers, reflection begins with better questions. Not questions to fix yourself, but to feel yourself. Not to find who you should be — but to return to who you already are beneath the noise.

Reflection slows us down in a culture of speed. It reveals patterns we blindly repeat. It helps us pause between action and reaction — so that we may choose from awareness, not habit. Reflection is not about perfect answers. It is about sacred presence — with your thoughts, your past, your wounds, your wisdom.

Some answers may come. Some may not. But in asking — sincerely, silently — you reconnect with the one who lives beneath all roles.

•

Prompts to Sit with:

Write, pause, walk, breathe. Then return — not to the book, but to yourself.

1. What part of me have I outgrown, but still cling to?
2. What truth am I avoiding because it would change my life?
3. In what moments do I feel most like myself?
4. What masks am I wearing… and why?
5. What would it look like to live from my inner clarity, not outer pressure?
6. What role or identity am I holding that no longer brings peace?
7. When do I perform the most? What would happen if I stopped?

8. What ache in my heart have I never named aloud?
9. Where does my silence begin — in fear or in presence?
10. When did I last sit without trying to fix anything — just to feel?
11. What part of me is performative? And what part simply is?
12. What is asking to be let go... so the real can emerge?
13. What silence am I afraid to sit with?

Self-Awareness to Being Self Framework

A journey inward —

from seeing the self... to being *the Self.*

From Self Awareness to Being Self Framework

A Pathway to Wholeness

True transformation is not about becoming someone else. It is about uncovering the self that was always there — buried beneath conditioning, noise, and survival identities.

This journey isn't linear. It's not a checklist. It is a spiral — where each return inward reveals deeper layers of truth. And it often begins not with a spiritual breakthrough... but with a simple discomfort, a question, or a whisper from within.

What It Is

The Self-Awareness to Being Self Framework is a four-stage guide designed to help you move from simply identifying with your thoughts, emotions, and life roles into resting as the awareness in which everything arises. Rather than offering quick fixes or external techniques, it provides an inward path: first observing your immediate experience, then reflecting on its deeper roots, next dissolving limiting identities, and finally living from the pure presence that precedes all content.

Why It's Important

Most of us unconsciously merge our sense of self with shifting elements—our beliefs, moods, achievements, and social labels. This leads to stress when circumstances change, self-doubt when expectations aren't met, and a persistent feeling that something essential is missing. By systematically creating space around your own experience, this framework loosens the grip of reactive patterns. You begin to discover that true freedom isn't found in changing external conditions, but in disentangling from the very stories and identifications that generate tension

For Whom

This framework is designed for anyone feeling the pull of modern life's pressures and longing for genuine inner anchoring. It's especially relevant if you experience:

- **Repetitive Thought Loops & Mental Overload:** constant planning, worrying, or self-criticism.
- **Emotional Reactivity & Instability:** sudden mood swings, anxiety, or unresolved grief.
- **Chronic Stress & Burnout:** feeling overwhelmed by work, caregiving, or life demands.
- **Relationship Disconnection:** feeling isolated from loved ones or struggling to be truly seen.
- **Financial & Life Uncertainty:** concerns about job security, money pressures, or an unpredictable future.
- **Loss of Meaning & Direction:** questioning "Who am I really?" or feeling disconnected from purpose.

- **Identity Confusion:** over-identification with roles, titles, or external approval.
- **Collective Anxiety:** a background hum of worry about global events or societal shifts.
- **Spiritual Disconnection:** feeling cut off from something greater, struggling with doubt, or longing for deeper faith and guidance.

Let us walk through the stages:

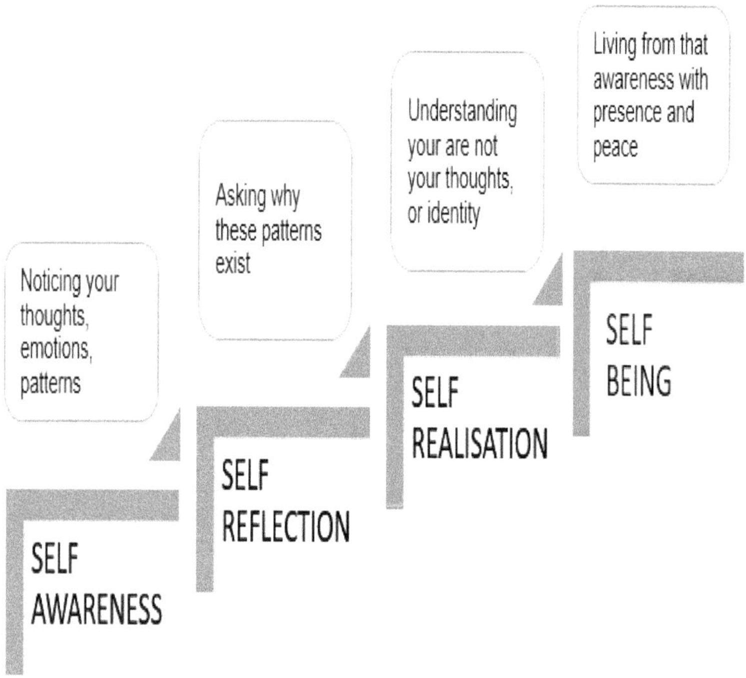

1. Self-Awareness – *The Awakening of Observation*

It begins the moment you catch yourself. You notice how you speak, how you react, how you avoid. You start to witness emotions without becoming them. You begin to *observe your anger*, instead of being consumed by it.
You *see your need for validation*, instead of blindly chasing it.

This is not about perfection. It's about the light turning on. It is the birth of the inner witness — a sacred turning point.

"I see now… that I have been on autopilot. And I no longer want to be."

- **Question to Explore:** "What is happening in me right now, without trying to change it?"
-
- **Activity:** Set a timer for 3–5 minutes. Sit quietly and label each experience as it surfaces (e.g., "thinking," "bored," "tension in shoulders"). No judgment—just naming.

2. Self-Reflection – *The Courage to Look Within*

Awareness leads to inquiry. You begin to ask: *Why?* Why does this trigger me? Why do I fear rest? Why do I keep repeating this cycle?

Here, reflection is not self-criticism. It's an act of love. It uncovers forgotten wounds, outdated beliefs, inherited fears. You realize: many of your reactions were never yours. They were adopted — from family, society, pain.

Now you begin to sit with your truth — not to fix it, but to understand it.

"I honor what shaped me, but I choose what guides me."

- **Question to Explore:** "What need, belief, or past experience lies behind this thought or feeling?"
-
- **Activity:** Choose one recurring thought or emotion. Write for five minutes in response to: "Why do I keep returning to this?" Notice any insights or shifts in perspective.

3. Self-Realization – *The Dissolving of Identity*

As you deepen in presence, a radical insight emerges:
You are not your story. You are not your roles, your thoughts, or your pain. You are that which sees it all — the unchanging presence beneath every changing experience.

This isn't philosophy. It is an inner knowing. A shift from *doing* to *being*. "I" am not this voice in my head. I am the silence it speaks into."

In this realization, fear starts losing its grip. You no longer seek worth — you remember it.

- **Question to Explore:** "If I am not this thought/feeling/role, then who or what am I?"
-
- **Activity:** During a brief pause in your day, close your eyes and ask yourself that question, then remain in silence. Notice what remains when the content of experience drops away.

4. Self-Being – *Living as Presence*

Now, the realization is lived. Not just in silence — but in action. You listen more, react less. You choose peace over pride. You work from love, not pressure. You lead without ego. You learn to rest in yourself — not to escape the world, but to engage it with clarity.

This stage isn't about detachment from life — it's about full engagement from inner alignment.

"I am here, now — not as a mask, but as truth in motion."

- **Question to Explore:** "How would I act right now if I were fully resting in presence?"
-
- **Activity:** Before any significant action—sending an email, entering a meeting, responding to a family member—take one conscious breath, recall your insight, and choose to respond from that inner calm.

•

A Gentle Return, Again and Again

You don't pass through these stages once. You return — in new moments, new triggers, new insights.
Each return deepens your presence and loosens the grip of the false self.

And in the end, you do not "become" something new.

You simply remember who you are, and live it.
You become a clear channel — of love, clarity, stillness, and courage.
You become — not more — but *whole*.

Integrated Daily Practices

Bringing awareness, reflection, realization, and presence into every dimension of life.

Below are eight mixed activities—each with a guiding question, followed by **possible solutions** to support integration and the **outcomes** you can expect over time.

1. <u>Body Scan & Release</u>

Question:
"Where am I holding tension in my body right now?"

Activity: Pause at midday. Close your eyes and do a slow head-to-toe scan, noticing any tightness or discomfort. Take three full breaths into each area, inviting release. Journal a brief note on what shifted.

Possible Solutions:

- **Progressive Muscle Relaxation:** Systematically tense and release muscle groups.
- **Gentle Yoga or Stretching:** Target areas of chronic tension.
- **Guided Body-Mind Meditation:** Use an app or recording that leads you through a full-body relaxation.

Outcomes:

- Reduced physical tension and pain
- Increased bodily awareness and ease
- Better posture and energy flow

---

2. Mindful Thought Observation

Question:
"Which thought patterns recur most often today?"

Activity:
Over the next hour, carry a small notebook. Each time a thought repeats (worry, judgment, planning), label it ("anxiety," "comparison") without engaging. At day's end, review which patterns surfaced most.

Possible Solutions:

- **Meditation Practice:** Daily 5–10 minutes of focused-attention meditation.
- **Thought Reframing:** Use cognitive journaling to challenge unhelpful thoughts.
- **MINDFUL PAUSE Technique:** Take three deep breaths before responding to recurring thoughts.

Outcomes:

- Clear data on habitual mental loops
- Reduced reactivity and rumination
- Enhanced ability to choose helpful thoughts

---

3. <u>Heart's Longing Check-In</u>

Question:
"What is my heart quietly asking for in this moment?"

Activity:
Place a hand over your heart for two minutes. Notice any subtle emotion—sadness, hope, gratitude. Name it mentally, then offer yourself a simple comfort (a glass of water, a stretch, a kind thought).

Possible Solutions:

- **Self-Compassion Meditation:** Practice loving-kindness phrases toward yourself.
- **Reflective Journaling:** Write a letter to your own heart acknowledging its needs.
- **Creative Expression:** Draw or paint the emotion you identify.

Outcomes:

- Greater self-nurturing and compassion
- Clarity on unmet emotional needs
- A warm sense of inner support

---

4. <u>Relationship Empathy Exercise</u>

Question:
"How might someone close to me be experiencing their own unseen burden?"

Activity:
Think of one person you interacted with today. Imagine their day from their perspective, considering stresses you don't know. Jot down one compassionate gesture or mental shift you can offer next time.

Possible Solutions:

- **Compassion Meditation:** Send them a silent wish of well-being.
- **Perspective Journaling:** Write a short paragraph "in their shoes."
- **Active Listening Practice:** Next conversation, reflect back what you hear.

Outcomes:

- Deepened empathy and connection
- Smoother, more supportive interactions
- Reduced conflict and misunderstanding

---

5. Vocation & Archetype Alignment

Question:
"What part of my work brings me alive, and what part feels robotic?"

Activity:
Identify one energizing task and one draining task. For each, note what inner quality (creativity, service, precision) was called forth, and how you might rebalance tomorrow.

Possible Solutions:

- **Strengths Assessment (DISC):** Clarify your primary style and align tasks accordingly.
- **Task Redesign:** Break draining tasks into smaller, meaningful steps.
- **Micro-breaks:** Insert 2-minute mindfulness or stretch breaks during robotic tasks.

Outcomes:

- Increased engagement and satisfaction
- Reduced work fatigue and burnout
- Clearer sense of purpose and flow

---

6. Mask Awareness Moment

Question:
"Which persona did I slip into when I felt insecure or judged?"

Activity:
Recall a moment you "performed." Write down which mask you wore—politeness, bravado, silence—and what you would have felt if you'd allowed your authentic response instead.

Possible Solutions:

- **Authenticity Journaling:** Explore fears behind that mask.
- **Role-Play Practice:** In a safe setting, practice expressing your true response.
- **Mirror Exercise:** Speak your authentic words while looking at your reflection.

Outcomes:

- Increased honesty and self-expression
- Deeper, more genuine connections
- Reduced emotional exhaustion from "performing"

---

7. Inner Dialogue Listening

Question:
"Which inner voice spoke the loudest today?"

Activity:
During a brief pause, close your eyes and listen to the first internal remark that arises. Is it the critic, caretaker, skeptic, or dreamer? Thank that voice for its intention, then shift focus to the silent observer for one minute.

Possible Solutions:

- **Dialoguing Technique:** Write a short dialogue between two inner voices.
- **Mindfulness Meditation:** Focus on the breath to stabilize the observer.
- **Compassionate Inquiry:** Ask each voice what it needs to feel safe.

Outcomes:

- Balanced inner conversation
- Reduced internal conflict
- Clearer guidance from deeper awareness

---

8. <u>Soul's Whisper Tracking</u>

Question:
"What subtle nudge or insight felt like it came from somewhere deeper?"

Activity:
At day's end, review your notes or journal. Highlight any unbidden inspirations. Choose one small action tomorrow that honors that deeper inner call.

Possible Solutions:

- **Quiet Meditation:** Sit for three breaths, tuning into that whisper.
- **Vision Journaling:** Sketch or write about what that insight feels like.
- **Accountability Pair:** Share your chosen action with a friend for gentle support.

Outcomes:

- Stronger alignment with inner purpose
- Increased trust in intuition
- More meaningful, soul-driven actions

Tip: You don't need to complete every practice each day. Instead, mix and match based on what resonates most. By combining these activities with targeted solutions—meditation, journaling, DISC insights, and mind-pattern analysis—you'll move from reaction to conscious presence in all areas of life.

Practices of Stillness

In stillness, I am not less… I am whole.

Before we step into the process of stillness, know that this section is here to guide you into the silent ground beneath your doing and thinking. Its purpose is simple yet profound: to help you meet the unshakable awareness that witnesses every breath, every emotion, every thought. In a culture that prizes productivity and equates silence with emptiness, you may find the mind rebelling, the heart craving distraction, and the body resisting pause. Yet it is precisely in these moments of quiet that clarity, resilience, and renewal are born. By learning to rest in stillness, you'll discover how to respond from presence rather than habit, transforming stress into insight and noise into peace. Ahead, you will explore three practices—Breath of Becoming, Journal: The Echo Within, and Daily Still Point—that offer gentle invitations to surrender into what already is and to remember the wisdom that always abides in the space of your being.

Breath of Becoming

Each morning, sit quietly. Let the spine rise like a tree, rooted in the earth, open to the sky. Whisper inwardly:

"I am... and yet I am not."
"Let me not just do — but be."

Take three deep, quiet breaths — not to change your state, but to remember your nature. Feel the breath not as effort, but as existence itself breathing you. Nothing to achieve. Nothing to perform. The inhale is not yours. The exhale is not controlled. You are simply witnessing — the breath, the awareness, the being.

This is not meditation as technique, but being as truth. In these breaths, the boundary between you and breath begins to fade. There is no center, no edge. Just a soft presence... being breathed.

Journal: The Echo Within

Before sleep, return to the self that watches all your daily masks with silent compassion. In your journal, complete:

- *"Today I wore the mask of…"*
- *"Beneath that, I truly felt…"*
- *"And in silence, I…"*

Let each line be a soft surrender — peeling back what you carried, without guilt, without resistance. What you wore is not wrong. What you felt is not shameful. And what you discovered in the silence — that is the pearl hidden in all illusion. This is not confession. It is release. A gentle offering of the day back to the source. When words run out, let your pen rest.

Do not judge. Do not fix. Simply witness. This is not for catharsis — but for clarity. You are not these masks. Not even the feelings beneath them. You are the awareness that holds them all — untouched, untroubled, infinite. Let yourself be seen — by no one but the stillness within.

In writing, the mind slows. The self becomes transparent. And the silence between words begins to speak. Let this nightly echo be a mirror, not of who you think you are — but of the stillness watching all identities rise and fall.

Daily Still Point

Choose at least one sacred minute each day. Not to achieve stillness, but to meet it. Set aside your devices, your thoughts, your doing. Be still. No phone, No task, Just pause, Sit, Breathe. Don't fix your posture. Don't fix your thoughts. Just surrender.

Let go of the need to become calm.
Let go of the need to "do it right."
Let go of the idea of "you" watching.
Let go.

Without agenda. Who remains when there's nothing to hold onto? What arises when even seeking stops? This is your Still Point. It's about presence. Whether you feel peace or chaos, it doesn't matter — both are held in the vast space of awareness. And that awareness is your true nature. Silent. Spacious. Free.

Thank you for walking this spiral of self with me. 💭

In silence, we become whole again. 🙏

Closing Reflections

Congratulations — not for arriving, but for remembering your way home.

Your Journey Continues from Here

This book may end,
But your awakening has only just begun.
You did not merely read these words —
You *walked through* them.
You met yourself in mirrors, roles, aches, silences.
And that takes courage.

A Soft Congratulations

You've done something
Most people avoid their whole lives —
You've turned inward, sat with truth,
And faced your own reflection.
That is worth celebrating — not with noise,
But with deep, nourishing *pause*.

TRANSFORMATION: REAL STORIES OF INNER RETURN

Across time, traditions, and professions — there are those who dared to pause, reflect, and surrender their surface identities to discover the vastness within. Their roles varied, but their return was the same: inward.

Gautama Buddha – The King Who Left to Awaken

Born a prince, Siddhartha Gautama had every worldly luxury. But the sight of suffering broke open a deeper question in him: *What is the root of all human sorrow?*
He left his palace, status, and name — not out of despair, but **longing**. After years of meditation and silence under the Bodhi tree, he awoke not as a prince, not as a prophet, but as **Truth realized**.

"***The mind is everything. What you think, you become.***

Guru Nanak Dev Ji – The Song of Ek Onkar *(Sikhism)*

Born in a time of religious divides, Guru Nanak walked across lands not to convert — but to awaken. He sang the Oneness of the Creator and the created.

"Ek Onkar. There is but One.

The same light shines in all." He urged simplicity, seva, inner listening, and truthful living. His revolution was not external — it was in consciousness: **merge ego into love**.

Jesus Christ – Love Beyond the Cross

Born in a humble manger, Jesus lived not for fame, but for **compassion**. He spoke in parables, healed the broken, and forgave even in death.
His transformation was not of role, but **radiance** — love that burns through separation.

"The Kingdom of God is within you."

Nisargadatta Maharaj – The Cigarette Seller Who Became a Sage

A humble shopkeeper in Mumbai, Nisargadatta wasn't born into mysticism. He asked one question with sincerity:

Who am I?

His teacher gave him a pointer. He clung to it like fire. Years later, he became one of the clearest voices in
Advaita Vedanta. "Wisdom tells me I am nothing. Love tells me I am everything."

Ramana Maharshi – The Boy Who Died to Be Reborn

At 16, Ramana faced death — not by circumstance, but by inner inquiry.

"***Who am I?***"

He asked, not philosophically, but directly — and never returned to ignorance. He lived simply, often silent, yet radiated a stillness that drew seekers across the globe."The Self is not somewhere far off. It is here and now."

Rumi (Sufi Mystic) – The Lover of the Beloved

Jalaluddin Rumi, after meeting his master Shams, turned from scholar to mystic. His verses speak of a love so deep, it consumes all ego:

"***You were born with wings, why prefer to crawl through life?"***

In Islam's spiritual branches, Rumi echoes the **unseen garden** within — where union with the Divine is not found in rules, but in surrender.His path was not escape from the world — but melting into the Beloved **within**.

Srila Prabhupada – Devotion as a Revolution

At age 69, with little money and great faith, Srila Prabhupada sailed to the West. Amid the 1960s chaos of war and rebellion, he carried only the **name of Krishna** and the purity of bhakti.
He transformed thousands not through dogma, but through **devotional love**, reminding the world that joy isn't outside — it's in *remembrance* of the divine within.

"Chant and be happy."

Acharya Mahapragya – The Silent Seer of Ahimsa *(Jainism)*

As the tenth Acharya of the Jain Terapanth order, he mastered not just scriptures, but **inner restraint**. Through *Preksha Dhyana* and *Anuvrat* movements, he taught that **violence begins in thought**, not action.

"Conquer the self, and you conquer the world."

His transformation was a gradual flowering — from discipline to detachment to deep compassion. He proved that **liberation begins with self-purification**.

BK Shivani – Stillness with a Smile

From corporate life to conscious life, her journey reflects gentle depth. In a loud world, she teaches the quiet power of **inner choice**.

"***Everything begins with a thought. Choose peace.***"

Her message isn't dramatic. It's daily. And it transforms.

Christian Monks – Silence as Worship

In monasteries from Assisi to Egypt, men and women chose the quiet path. Figures like **Thomas Merton**, **St. Francis of Assisi**, and **Mother Teresa** served not to preach — but to embody love. Merton wrote:

"We are not at peace with others because we are not at peace with ourselves."

Their transformation came not from doctrines, but through surrender, silence, and **Christ-consciousness** — a living love.

His Holiness the Dalai Lama - The Compassion That Transcends Borders (Tibetan Buddhism)

Exiled from his homeland, holding the pain of a nation, the Dalai Lama chose not hate, but **compassion**.

"My religion is very simple. My religion is kindness."

He lives not as a ruler, but as a humble monk — embodying equanimity. His transformation is not dramatic. It is **daily**, filled with gentle discipline and immense empathy.In every smile, he teaches this: Peace is not a place. It is a practice.

Radhanathan Swami - The Journey Within

From the streets of Chicago to the caves of the Himalayas, his search wasn't outward — it was always inward. In *The Journey Within*, he shares that true fulfillment arises not by conquering the world, but by discovering the soul.

His path reminds us: When the heart kneels, the spirit rises.

Lao Tzu – The Master of the Unforced Path *(Taoism)*

Author of the *Tao Te Ching*, Lao Tzu did not preach religion — he whispered of the invisible current beneath all life.

"Knowing others is intelligence; knowing yourself is true wisdom. Mastering others is strength; mastering yourself is true power."

He taught Wu Wei — effortless action in alignment with the Tao. His message:
Be like water — humble, yielding, yet unstoppable.

Osho Rajneesh – The Rebel Who Pointed to Stillness

Osho broke traditions, challenged norms, and invited the world into **awareness without bondage**. His journey was never about rejecting the world — but dissolving the false in it.

"Be realistic: Plan for a miracle."

"The moment you accept yourself, you become beautiful."

Premanandji Maharaj – The Innocence of the Heart

From a young boy reciting katha, to a spiritual guide glowing with childlike purity, Premanandji teaches not with weighty words, but with a light that melts defenses. His tears during bhajans, his joy in divine stories, reflect a soul not performing — but **surrendered**.
His transformation is not of logic, but of love., bliss.

Rabbi Nachman of Breslov – The Mystic of Joy Amidst Shadows *(Judaism – Hasidic)*

A mystic born of exile and sorrow, Rabbi Nachman wept and danced in the same breath. His teachings were not of law, but of the **living heart**.

"The whole world is a very narrow bridge, but the main thing is not to be afraid."

He urged radical joy, honest tears, and daily dialogue with God. His inner transformation was simple: **from brokenness to boundless connection.**

Sadhguru – From Business to Boundlessness

Before he became a spiritual icon, **Sadhguru Jaggi Vasudev** was a successful entrepreneur. But one afternoon, he sat on a rock and had a profound spiritual awakening. He left everything, not out of suffering, but because he realized:

"The only thing that's yours is the inner dimension."

Today, he blends leadership with **consciousness**, reminding the world that outer growth means little without inner expansion.

Zen Masters – The Laugh of the Empty Mind

Masters like **Hakuin**, **Bankei**, and **Thich Nhat Hanh** didn't teach answers — they taught how to be present to the question.A monk once asked a master, "What is the path?" He replied, "The everyday mind is the way."

Zen is not theory. It is nowness.

It is waking up from the dream of identity to the stillness beneath.

Acharya Prashant – Truth with Fire

From IIM to inquiry, Acharya Prashant questions identity like a sword. He offers clarity, not comfort.

"Truth doesn't comfort the ego — it dissolves it."

His transformation is living proof: intellectual brilliance becomes luminous only when it bows to inner wisdom.

Dale Carnegie – The Salesman Who Found the Human Heart

Known for *How to Win Friends and Influence People*, Dale Carnegie once struggled with anxiety and failure. He transformed not through theory, but through a deep curiosity for what people truly feel. His teachings, though pragmatic, are grounded in empathy, respect, and inner understanding — rare in business literature.

"When dealing with people, remember you are not dealing with creatures of logic, but with creatures of emotion."

Indigenous Wisdom – The Earth as Mirror of the Soul *(Native / Tribal Spirituality)*

Across continents — from Aboriginal Dreamtime to Native American sacred circles — the teaching is the same:

"We are not owners of the earth. We are part of her breath."

Shamans, elders, and medicine women don't "preach" — they listen. To wind, fire, river, grief. Their inner return is through rhythm, ritual, and reverence. They teach that **divinity is not only above — it is *beneath* your feet.**

Mo Gawdat – The Engineer Who Chose Joy

After losing his son, this Google executive could've broken. Instead, he went inward. Wrote *Solve for Happy*, and shared wisdom built on grief-transformed-love.

"Pain is real. Suffering is optional."

"Happiness is not a result of what life gives you. It's a result of how you think about what life gives you."

Naval Ravikant - From Hustle to Inner Stillness

Tech investor and founder of AngelList, Naval is known for wealth creation strategies. But he often speaks of something deeper:

"A calm mind, a fit body, and a house full of love. These things cannot be bought. They must be earned."

Naval moved from hustle culture to deep introspection. Through self-inquiry, he dismantled old mental patterns and found that **freedom isn't success — it's self-awareness.**

Ratan Tata - Grace in Action

Ratan Tata, the iconic industrialist, carried the Tata legacy forward with unmatched dignity. In interviews, he often reflects quietly, without fanfare. What sets him apart isn't just what he built — it's what he didn't let ego destroy. Known for his emotional intelligence and silent philanthropy, he once said:

"I don't believe in taking right decisions. I take decisions and then make them right."

His path reflects a deep trust in intuition and service — more than a hunger for control.

Ray Dalio – The Billionaire Who Meditates to Think Clearly

Founder of Bridgewater Associates, Ray Dalio built an empire on logic and analytics. But beneath the spreadsheets was a soul seeking stillness.

"Meditation has been the single most important reason for whatever success I've had."

He discovered that clarity doesn't just come from control — but from **quietness**. Now, each morning, he sits in silence, not to escape the world, but to lead within it.

Tony Robbins – From Pain to Purpose to Presence *(Global Transformation Coach)*

Born in chaos, raised in hardship, Tony Robbins became the voice of empowerment for millions. But behind the peak-state energy was a man who had to confront his own emotional shadows.
Through deep neuro-emotional work, fasting retreats, and silent reflection, Tony discovered:

"Success without fulfillment is the ultimate failure."

Today, he teaches not just how to achieve — but how to live with gratitude, grace, and grounded self awareness. The most powerful part of his work? **Helping others meet the parts of themselves they've hidden.**

The Author himself – Remembering Over Becoming

Entrepreneur, Working Professional, Visionary, Seeker. He spent years in pursuit of purpose — building ventures, studying deep disciplines, mentoring minds. Yet, beneath all the movement, a still voice asked:

"Who am I beneath all I'm trying to become?"
He had read the words of saints, studied with masters, and spoken on leadership. But the real turning point wasn't external — it was internal. A quiet realization arose:

"I don't need to add more to myself. I need to remember what was never lost."

From that space, he began to shift — not by leaving his life, but by infusing it with presence. Through weekly journaling, reflection, and moments of solitude, he came home to his essence:
Not just the doer. Not just the dreamer. But the witness.

His story is one of reclaiming the self *within* the world, not apart from it. Today, he continues to lead — not by striving to be more, but by being more truly himself.

✨ And Many More...

They may never speak on a stage, or publish a book,
But in quiet corners of the world,
Mothers, monks, artists, healers, teachers, workers, wanderers —
are waking up from the noise of becoming...
And returning to the stillness of **being**.
This book is for them. For you. For all of us —
Who have tried everything outside,
And are now ready to come home.

One Flame, Many Lamps

From Himalayas to Hollywood,
From the fire-walkers to forest-dwellers,
From monks in robes to coaches in suits —
They all speak one silent truth:
You are not just the roles you play.
You are the one who watches.
You are awareness. You are love.
You are... and yet you are not.
Let this book be your still mirror in a noisy world.
Let these stories remind you: the world's greatest pilgrimage is not to a place —
But to the **presence within you**.

The Common Thread

Whether billionaire or monk, tech leader or teacher — the real return is always the same. **Inward.**
Where ambition meets stillness,
Where roles dissolve into essence,
Where doing bows to being.

ONE LIGHT, MANY PATHS – THE INNER CALL OF ALL TRADITIONS

Across nations, scriptures, and tongues, a single whisper echoes: *Go within.* Whether through devotion, stillness, surrender, or self-inquiry, the essence remains — the Divine is not distant. It is closer than breath, more silent than thought, and forever present in the heart.

This section gathers the purest gems from spiritual traditions across the world, all pointing to love, compassion, and the inner journey to the Self.

Bhagavad Gita (Hinduism)
"One who sees all beings in the Self, and the Self in all beings, never turns away from It."

— ***Bhagavad Gita 6.29***

"Lift yourself by yourself; do not degrade yourself. The Self alone is the friend of the Self, and the Self alone is the enemy of the Self."

— ***Bhagavad Gita 6.5***

Bible (Christianity)
"The Kingdom of God is within you."

— ***Luke 17:21***

"Love your neighbor as yourself."

— ***Mark 12:31***

Quran (Islam)
"We are closer to him than [his] jugular vein."

— ***Surah Qaf 50:16***

"Indeed, in the remembrance of Allah do hearts find rest."

— ***Surah Ar-Ra'd 13:28***

Guru Granth Sahib (Sikhism)
"The One who created the creation is within the creation."

— Ang 83

"See the Divine Light within all, and you will never forget the Beloved Lord."

— Ang 599

Dhammapada (Buddhism)
"All that we are is the result of what we have thought."

— Verse 1

"Conquer anger with non-anger; conquer badness with goodness."

— Verse 223

Jainism (Agamas & Sutras)
"One who disregards nature disregards his own existence which is entwined with it."

"Ahimsa Paramo Dharma" — Non-violence is the highest religion.

— Acharanga Sutra

Tao Te Ching (Taoism)

"Knowing others is intelligence; knowing yourself is true wisdom."

— Chapter 33

"The softest thing in the world overcomes the hardest."

— Chapter 78

Judaism (Torah & Kabbalah)

"The soul of man is the lamp of the Lord, searching all the innermost parts."

— Proverbs 20:27

"The light of the Infinite is within every soul."

— Zohar, Bereshit

Sufi Mysticism (Islam)

"Your task is not to seek for love, but to find all the barriers within yourself that you have built against it."

— Rumi, Masnavi

"You were born with wings — why prefer to crawl through life?"

— Rumi

Bahá'í Faith

"Possess a pure, kindly and radiant heart."

— ***Gleanings, Section 1***

"The betterment of the world can be accomplished through pure and goodly deeds."

— ***Bahá'u'lláh***

Indigenous Traditions

"We are all related"

— ***Mitákuye Oyás'iŋ (Lakota)***

"Do not look outside yourself for the leader. We are the ones we've been waiting for."

— ***Hopi Elders***

Advaita Vedanta (Non-Dualism)

"Aham Brahmāsmi — I am Brahman."

— ***Brihadaranyaka Upanishad 1.4.10***

"Tat Tvam Asi — Thou art That."

— ***Chandogya Upanishad 6.8.7***

Sanātana Dharma (The Eternal Path)
"Atma is the friend and the enemy of the Self."

— ***Bhagavad Gita 6.5***

"Dharma protects those who protect Dharma."

— ***Manusmriti 8.15***

The One Message:

In every tongue, through every teacher, the Eternal whispers the same truth —

Go within. Love deeply. Realize the Self. And see all as One.

AUTHOR'S NOTE

This short book is not a teaching — it is a remembering. It is not meant to impress the mind, but to embrace the soul. 🌟

We are all becoming, unbecoming, dissolving and rediscovering. Every name we wear, every mask we hold, every ache we hide — they are not wrong. They are doors. This book is not an escape from the world, but a returning to the self within the world. 💫

If even one line made you pause… not for answer, but for presence — then the purpose is fulfilled. 🌿

— Abhishek Garg

ABOUT THE AUTHOR

Abhishek Garg is not just a writer — he is a witness of life's silences, a seeker of truth, and a soul devoted to the unseen essence behind all things.

Founder of the **Supreme Parinaman Foundation**, Abhishek's life bridges the inner and outer worlds — blending the wisdom of spiritual inquiry with the compassion of service and the precision of poetic expression.

His words rise not from theory but from deep reflection, lived paradoxes, and quiet conversations with the divine. He walks the path of presence — not as a master, but as a fellow traveler who has known confusion, clarity, collapse, and calling.

With a background spanning business, transformation work, and spiritual research, Abhishek now serves through writing, guiding, and creating spaces where others may reconnect with their truth.

This book is not his first word — and certainly not his last.
It is a still point in his journey, shared with open hands and a whisper of hope:
"May you remember what you never truly forgot."

A LETTER TO THE WORLD

For much of my life, I searched for myself in definitions—names, roles, identities others could understand. I measured my worth through what I gave, what I achieved, or how well I fit into the expectations laid out before me. But somewhere along the way, something in me softened. Or perhaps it broke open.

I began to sense a deeper truth: that I am not just one thing. Not just one thought, feeling, or label. "I am… and yet I am not" I am form, and I am formless. I am the seeker, and I am the stillness underneath the seeking.

And as I discovered this, I also began to see you, dear world, in a new way. Not just as countries and people and noise—but as a shared soul, fragmented across many hearts. I saw pain in your eyes, the kind that never got spoken. I saw joy you weren't sure you deserved. I saw resilience masked as routine. And in all of it, I recognized something deeply human… something deeply divine.

So this book is my quiet offering to you. A prayer in the form of pages. A mirror for what's been hidden under the surface. A reminder that even if we've never met, even if your path looks different than mine—still, we are connected.

I offer you this love, not because I know your whole story, but because I recognize your essence. You are worthy of being seen. Of being held. Of being reminded that you don't need to earn your belonging. You already belong.

May this book meet you where you are. And may it whisper to the part of you that already knows the way home.

With love,
The One Who Walks with You in the Mystery

FURTHER STEPS

Encouragement for the Road Ahead

- You may forget these truths. That's okay. Return to them.
- You may ache again. That's okay. Feel through it — not away from it.
- You may get lost again. That's okay. You now know the direction of home.

This isn't the end of the book — it's a **beginning of deeper being**.

Stay Connected

Share your reflections, moments, or questions at:
supremeparinamanfoundation@gmail.com

Explore new writings, meditations, or community sessions at:
www.linkedin.com/company/supreme-parinaman-foundation-spf

Use **#SupremeParinamanFoundation, #SPF** to share your journey on social platforms.

Invite Others In

If this book touched you, help it reach those who need a hand back to themselves:
Gift it to a friend who hides their tears behind smiles

- Quote a passage in your journal or blog

- Lead a soul-circle where people read and reflect together

You don't have to be a teacher to light the way. You just have to be *honest* about your path.

Support the Mission

Every book you share helps us bring spiritual poetry, inner healing, and soulful resources to communities that are often forgotten by the mainstream world.

Support, or collaborate at:

www.linkedin.com/company/supreme-parinaman-foundation-spf

supremeparinamanfoundation@gmail.com

FINAL WHISPER

Congratulations for being

brave enough to feel.

To listen. To pause.

To be more than your name.

May this book stay close to your

breath.

And may your breath stay close to

your truth. The spiral home has

begun.

You are not alone anymore.

www.ingramcontent.com/pod-product-compliance
Ingram Content Group UK Ltd.
Pitfield, Milton Keynes, MK11 3LW, UK
UKHW021339190726
13845UKWH00027B/622

9 789334 336061